Wholehearted *Wonder* Women 50^{PLUS}

Wholehearted Wonder Women 50 PLUS

Courage, Confidence, & Creativity at Any Age

Lulu Trevena

Featuring

Heidi Blair • Ghislaine Bouskila • Daniela Caine • Corinne Coppola • Laura Di Franco
Françoise Everett • Bridgette Graham-Barlow • Liz Hanzi • Nancy Jones • Keren Kilgore
Wanda Knisley • Sandra Leoni • Rika Rivka Markel • Pat Perrier • Joy Resor
Meredith Sims • Kelley Storum • Mi Straznicky • Julie Ulstrup • Yantra-ji • Dr. Zora

*Your words will change the world
when you're brave enough to share them.*
www.BraveHealer.com
(703)915-3653
Facebook: @BraveHealerbyLaura
Instagram: @BraveHealerProductions
Twitter: @Brave_Healer

Lulu Trevena supports women to be confident and creative at any age. She offers Soulful Living Coaching and Quantum Healing globally and virtually. Lulu's passion is wrapping her diverse life experience into events and programs. She is an advocate for women, creative living, and self-expression. Her beautiful books and card deck are special gifts for those you love and cherish.

Connect here: **www.livelifewithwonder.com**

DEDICATION

I dedicate this book to my rich matriarchal lineage. My mother and my grandmother greatly influenced my life. To my daughters, who have repeatedly pointed me toward the depth of my heart. To the women of all ages in my family, past, present, and future.

This is my offering, along with my sisterhood of co-authors, to those who seek to nurture and expand their wholeheartedness in an embodied and self-respectful way. Living with confidence, courage, creativity, and wonder in our fifties and beyond, we are helping change the societal narrative of women and age together, and with the support of some good men. We stand proud, candidly.

To the courageous who have lived life experiences that helped secure their confidence and honor their emotions.

To the seekers, may you joyously stumble across what you seek, whilst embodying your own wisdom.

To the creatives, which means every human soul, because to live life is one of the most creative pursuits there is.

We acknowledge and celebrate you, the creative, courageous, confident woman!

*Women are the most powerful force on the planet. We drive industries, love, and heal our families and communities. We're leaders, lovers, and friends. But culture and upbringing have caused so many to dim their power and talents. As we hit a certain age, different for each of us, we reach a point where we recognize the beauty of our experiences, our wisdom, and even the lines in our faces. That is our awakening. The first steps may be a little tenuous, but as we take them, we stop apologizing for our strength and begin to truly clothe ourselves in our innate power. **Wholehearted Wonder Women 50 Plus** is a beautiful collaboration and guide on our personal journeys and in our roles as mentors and teachers for others. It's filled with strong women, sharing themselves and their wisdom with each other and with the next generations. As we contribute to each other, we all become wiser, stronger, more peaceful, and joyful. Through that sharing, we lift each other, our families, and communities.*

Deberah Bringelson, Global Business Growth Authority and Empowerment Expert. One of the most profit-producing business growth authorities and empowerment experts in the world, Deberah Bringelson is best known for her work with Richard Branson and for helping companies in 17 countries grow 100% to 3,546% in under 12 months. Forbes Coaches Council Official Member.
Website: https://deberahbringelson.com/
LinkedIn: https://www.linkedin.com/in/deberah/

This book is a poetic and heart-full invitation to beauty, wonder, and grace, an invitation through story, intimacy, and the wisdom of experience to jump into your calling and walk through the door of aging being all of who you were meant to be.

To be in the presence of these women, their collective wisdom, and soulful sharing, is to take your own seat in the circle of womanhood, in the circle of life, present, embodied, grace-filled, and flowering.

David Bedrick, J.D. Dipl. PW, author of *You Can't Judge a Body by Its Cover* and *Talking Back to Dr. Phil*
Website: https://www.davidbedrick.com
Facebook: https://www.facebook.com/DBedrick

This book is a gathering of global friendship and you are welcomed in wholeheartedly. Lulu warmly greets us and masterfully creates a circle of women to hold us as we move through the book. As we read each chapter, we meet each woman as she stands in the center with her heart on her sleeve and shares her journey with us. Each woman, one by one, lets us see into the hardest moments of their lives and the opening to wisdom that gave them back to themselves. Not only do we feel like we are sitting in the blessed company of heartfelt, brave, conscious, and courageous women, we are held by them ~ by their commitment to our wellbeing, our growth, our joy from the same place of grace that they acquired theirs.

This is a masterful gathering of women's wisdom ~ not only do we get to meet and be in the company of these powerful and committed women, each of them have offered us a gift of love. This is not merely a wonderful book, it is a "how to" book with gifts of a love offering in every chapter. Rich and full of beautiful practices, there are specific ways to be in touch with yourself and your divinity, to touch your life from creativity, to self-healing, to grief release, to holistic fashion, meditation and far beyond. Enjoy this book and after you have savored it for now, tuck it somewhere safe to refer again when you need a remedy for whatever ails you along your adventure of life, love, courage and creativity.

Katherine McClelland is an author, Spiritual Psychologist, and an Ordained Minister of Universal Spirituality. She is a Certified Relationship and Mind/Body Coach, a Transformational Leader and Licensed Coach and Trainer of Partnership Mastery.

Website: https://katherinemcclelland.com/

Facebook: https://www.facebook.com/katherine.mcclelland.18/

Wholehearted Wonder Women 50 Plus encourages you to highlight, underline, write in the margins. Use those fancy pens and all the colors! Come back again and again as time and need warrant. You will want this book easily at hand. The cover art is stunning; the words inside are simultaneously poetic and pragmatic. It's a must-read.

Kami Guildner, host of Extraordinary Women Ignite Conference and Extraordinary Women Radio, best-selling author of *Firedancer: Your Spiral Journey to a Life of Passion & Purpose*
Website: https://www.kamiguildner.com/
Facebook: https://www.facebook.com/kamiguildnercoaching/

This inspiring wholehearted book, will guide you to let go of your baggage, honor your inner gifts, and move into the most empowering time of your life.

Rachael Jayne Groover, Founder of The Awakened School and Best-selling author of *Powerful and Feminine: How to Increase your Magnetic Presence and Attract the Attention You Want* and *Divine Breadcrumbs: A Search for True Love and Enlightenment*
Website: http://theawakenedschool.com/
Facebook: Facebook.com/RachaelJayneGroover

What a gift! Once you pick this book up, it's difficult to put it down. The authors of each chapter talk about their own lives, real-life women telling you stories that are relatable, true, intimate, and honest. The authentic feeling comes right off the page. You can skip from one chapter to another or sit down and read from the intro to the last page. Your choice, you will want to spend time with each chapter and use the tools provided. As well, Lulu Trevena and the authors provide an intentional community across various social media platforms so you can contact them, engage in lively discussion, and join with other wonderful, wonder-filled women as you create the life you want, and the life you deserve.

Nita Patel, Best Selling Author, Artist, Speaker, Performance Coach.
Opulaunh, LLC
Website: https://www.nita-patel.com/
IG: @thenitapatel

Special Invitation to the Reader

Glorious women, your stories and adventures have created this grand, exquisite tapestry called your life. May this book offer additional support, honor you, and remind you of your wholeheartedness and wonder-spark at this next phase of your journey. No matter what has happened in your past—illness, hardships, loss, and betrayals—know that you have immense capacity within you to move forward with empowerment.

Please use this book as a reclamation of the all-ness of you and the cultivation of your own spark of wonder, which cannot be bought or bargained for but is the richest of prizes to grant yourself. Wonder Woman you, your way!

Opportunities and challenges are part of our *shero's* journey. Let this book offer you a healing balm and deep resonance in the stories shared. Inside are more resources, tools, and awareness that you can massage where needed for comfort.

Our bodies have a natural aging pattern. We will face changes in health, lifestyle, relationships, and in the amount of time or energy we have to do these things.

I like the image of a spiral path. Sometimes we are moving up, sometimes we are moving down, and sometimes we are just resting until we know the next logical, aligned, or soul-enriching step. Life is not linear. Welcome the all-ness and be open to the journey.

I've invited some very special women to be part of this book and their wisdom and insights have enriched me. I encourage you to connect with the authors, read their stories and use their tools. Live into their shared teachings and the blessings they offer with their words, skills, and hearts.

Join our global community on Facebook The Wholehearted Wonder Women 50 plus Global Community

https://www.facebook.com/groups/154614839857015/

The greatest asset in your life is your own inner awareness and self-care. It is not a luxury; it's a necessity—your life matters. You matter.

Like a sunflower following the sun, we know what can sustain life...let us turn toward that energy.

We learn and become aware of saboteurs and naysayers; both inner and outer...let us protect our self with good boundaries.

We are enriched by the manure that feeds and guides us towards growth... let us cultivate the learnings.

May we blossom in our own unique way—with wonder, fire, passion, and most importantly, as allies.

DISCLAIMER

This book offers wellness information and is designed for educational purposes only. You should not rely on this information as a substitute for, nor does it replace professional medical advice, diagnosis, or treatment. If you have any concerns or questions about your health, you should always consult with a physician or other healthcare professional. Do not disregard, avoid, or delay obtaining medical or health-related advice from your healthcare professional because of something you may have read here. The use of any information provided in this book is solely at your own risk.

Developments in medical research may impact the wellness advice that appears here. No assurances can be given that the information contained in this book will always include the most relevant findings or developments with respect to the particular material.

Having said all that, know that the experts here have shared their tools, practices, and knowledge with you with a sincere and generous intent to assist you on your wellness journey. Please contact them with any questions you may have about the techniques or information they provided. They will be happy to assist you further!

CONTENTS

INTRODUCTION

Wholehearted *whole·heart·ed* | \ ˈhōl-ˈhär-təd \

1: completely and sincerely devoted, determined, or enthusiastic

2: marked by complete earnest commitment: free from all reserve or hesitation

I love Brené Brown's meaning for wholehearted living in her book, *The Gifts of Imperfection.*

"Wholehearted living is about engaging in our lives from a place of worthiness. It means cultivating the courage, compassion, and connection to wake up in the morning and think, *No matter what gets done and how much is left undone, I am enough.* It's going to bed at night thinking, *Yes, I am imperfect and vulnerable and sometimes afraid, but that doesn't change the truth that I am also brave and worthy of love and belonging.*"

Wonder *won·der* | \ ˈwən-dər \

1a: a cause of astonishment or admiration

b: MIRACLE

2: the quality of exciting, amazed admiration

3: rapt attention or astonishment at something awesomely mysterious or new to one's experience

Pure intentionality is how this book was birthed. I dig words; they have a texture and emotionality. I named my business Live Life with Wonder shortly after I gave birth to my third child, Lila Persia, when I was 41. When she was two, I was admiring her joyous wonder as she looked at the small stones she picked up. I said to myself, *children live with so much wonder, I wished adults could too!* This still clear voice inside of me encouraged, *register the business name*

Live Life with Wonder. I had no idea that living life with wonder was mine yet to claim in so many ways.

Over the last two decades, I have been a yoga teacher, quantum healer, coach, women's group facilitator, and author: all these have an essence of wholeness or healing and wonder.

For decades, as women, we have found ourselves giving and perhaps even over-giving to others. Much of this has been its own reward and comes from our innate natural nurturing approach to life.

Working with women in circles for decades, I have heard stories; far too many stories of giving our power away, not being appreciated, and even feeling that what we did had no value. I have heard stories of trying to be Super Woman or Super Mum and the anguish that there was never a mark to reach that felt acceptable, even when the cape was donned.

Let me shine the light on you.

I want you to be Wonder Woman for yourself and *only* for yourself. It is time you cease trying to be that for others.

No cape needed. No armor required.

Leather bodice, skirt, boots, armbands, headband, and gold belt are optional! At times I choose to adorn myself with some of these and dress as Wonder!

Wholehearted Wonder Women: Us. You and me, unabashedly living our life in its fullness and delight.

If you have been feeling like you have been running on empty for far too long, unsure what you want, or unclear about what the next steps on your journey look like, may our authors offer signposts to guide and illuminate the path for you.

I like that this time of our life, is often referred to as the Golden Age. Gold has the essence of luxury and preciousness.

Three months before I got married my mother died. She was only 58. It was a time of confusion, anger, and grieving jumbled with joy and celebration. I was angry she had not stayed long enough to see me get married and angry at myself for not involving her more in the preparations. Our deep emotions often live side by side competing with one another in a cacophony and requiring us to straddle them in a seesaw motion. Mine certainly did.

In 2020 I turned 58. I was my Mum's age when she departed. I looked at my life and realized the rich delight of living in my body and the depth of wisdom I'd gained over the years. I also saw how much vitality, passion, and purpose I still had for life! Our time to leave is unknown. And for many of us, the death of loved ones is a reminder of our mortality. Yet we often waste our time as if we have so much more of it left. Seize the day.

Each morning, I remind myself that I have a rich lived wisdom, to support my wonder-filled life forward. I listen to my soul's promptings; this is why I write. You can explore my other books at the back of this volume.

Welcome Wholehearted Wonder Women!

CHAPTER 1

If Not Now, When?!

Receiving Life with Grace, Wonder, and Awe

By Lulu Trevena, Artist, Quantum Healer, Soulful Living Coach, Art of Feminine Presence® Licensed Teacher Level 2

Life is not measured by the number of breaths you take but by the moments that take your breath away.

—Maya Angelou

My Story

"We have an opportunity to live in the USA," my husband said matter-of-factly. I looked at him dumbfounded and flatly replied, "I know I said I would live anywhere in the world with you, Bub, but I was not thinking the US, I was thinking somewhere richer with culture and art." That was nine years ago.

Our brains are wired for negativity! I don't say that to upset the mind-set people or the positive thinkers. It's more that when we understand the operating system, our own human operating system, we know what we have to work with and the best way to enrich our life's experiences. When we get to middle age, society has often stamped us with a certain way of being. It tells us how we're supposed to show up and often shows us where we are lacking. Historically, we have glorified youthful beauty and virility, and less so, wisdom and experience. While both are important, we are rewriting history and the age narrative.

I have never felt as old as I did lying on our high polished kitchen floor in pain, unable to move or speak in the dark early hours of the morning, a few months before my 55th birthday. Quiet cloaking me, fully laced in panic. "Mum, Mum, Mum, are you alright?" Our teenager called out (which seemed like an eternity) later. How long I had lain there, I am unsure; time stood still. She would later tell me she was unsure what the whimpering sound was, which somehow woke her up long before her school day alarm. "I thought it was a sick or dying animal," her voice small and shaky. I had never fainted in my life before that day. The first time I picked myself up, dazed, unsure what had happened, and then within minutes, I fainted for the second time. This time hitting my back on the kitchen island, leaving me crumpled wrapped around the domestic structure, shocked and winded, unable to call out, the rest of the house still asleep in Slumberville. Our youngest heard me and woke my husband, and an ambulance was summoned. I was in intense pain, crying, disheveled and disorientated, unable to move, and feeling small, vulnerable, and weak, like a sick animal. I, too, felt my whimperings through every cell.

In the hospital with a fractured spine, I realized something in my life had to change. I had been on a self-development path for years. I felt blessed and positive generally, yet I had a recurring dream of me like a small, soft, cuddly toy that was losing a trail of beads when I moved in any direction—losing my substance, life force, and essence. Between the crisp hospital sheets, my focus on my back, I came face to face with the question. *Who's got my back?* I wondered, *did my husband?*

I managed my pain with less medication, using all my learned healing tools and practices. Being unable to move gave me reflection time and ample healing opportunities. I was blessed to have people all over the world sending me distance healing and prayers. And within two days, I was free of medication, the pain endurable.

Accidents, pain, or disease are great motivators for us human beings, I have noticed. I was shaken out of the complacency that I was hiding behind and faced myself, ego naked. With brutal honesty and wholeheartedness, I asked myself, "Is this it, is this my life? Is it time to face what is not working? Lulu, what are you doing with your one glorious life?"

"Tell me, what is it you plan to do with your one wild and precious life?"
I was reminded of these beautiful words from Mary Oliver's poem and felt cradled with care whilst in pondering mode.

This was a reawakening moment for me. As a wife and mother, much of my life revolved around my family; my dreams and desires put on the back burner, awaiting fuel or stoking. Or had they been laid barren, wilted, flaccid? I had delayed my own projects and spiritual promptings as I was still in the caretaker role. Over my lifetime, I had heard the saying, *you can have it all!* For me, that played out as I had to wait until it was my turn (which had no clear date). Motherhood has been one of the richest, most rewarding, and soul-nourishing journeys I have had the greatest pleasure to take. I relish that. Yet, I was bargaining my happiness as less important than others, and I now wanted my throne!

Desire would not be quieted, and I was far from ready to sit on the porch in a rocker! My maternal grandmother lived until 104, and I, as the Live

Life with Wonder woman, knew she had a whole lot of wonder to get busy with living. Like a clock impatiently ticking, *"If Not Now, When?"* resounded.

Having it all means something different for every person. I encourage you to find out what it means to you, sweet reader. Allow yourself the grace to get lost in an enriching exploration or pursuit, where time feels luscious and your wonder and awe radiate.

As my spine strengthened, it was like creating a new structure. I started from the ground up. Like any good house, the foundation needs to be strong; the walls need to be upright and aligned before any decor gets placed. I listened more inwardly. I became more tender with myself. I asked with curiosity, "What do *I* want my next forty or fifty years to look and feel like?" I said *no* more to others; I said *yes* more to myself; I listened, I created, I journaled, I learned new skills that delighted me. From a young age, Lulu in first position was a foreign concept, but I was willing.

Our business sold a few years before; two decades of my husband's frontline hard work and my multi-faceted family and home reconnaissance resulted in a big monetary reward. The house was bought and owned outright in one payment. Two BMW convertibles side by side in the garage, mine sapphire blue. This was my 50th year. Life had a new meaning and freedom. Flashy is not my style. I am much more Earth Mother in my essence and modern hippie in my clothing choice. This new lifestyle had to have humility and humbleness at its heart.

We called the USA home just months before, a mammoth move from Australia with two teenagers, an eight-year-old, and a cat; a new decade, a new land, a new life.

Grief and excitement side by side again. The inner pangs in my heart stretched out through my whole being. Moving away in this fifth decade from my supportive community, years built on shared interests, our daughters' childhood stomping grounds fading in the distance, and feeling like the standing I had in our community was leaving a giant void. *Who the fuck was I now?*

I value community like air. I found myself gasping, my airways restricted.

We've all heard sayings like *home is where the heart is*, or *you create home wherever you go*. I have done this numerous times: it is a honed skill. With ease and grace, I created homes and communities many times. We've moved multiple times, including out of Sydney five years earlier. This was very different. I was in the beginning of my 50's starting over in a new country. The task was feeling like a burden, to prove myself in an ocean of unfamiliar faces and more unfamiliar hearts.

I have the volunteer gene. I support, I contribute, and I pride myself on getting jobs done. I involve myself in communities this way; it works well for them and me. I often take on the job no one else will, even when the proverbial to-do list is full. I've been known for having room for yet another project or job in support of someone else, first! The agitated voice in my head was making a ruckus, and her inner critic language was all shades of colorful cussing. And loud. *What about me? What the fuck about me?* It vibrated incessantly like a jackhammer intrusive on a Sunday morning.

A few years after this, I named my critical inner voice in a women's retreat. She had been with me all my life. Yes, you have one too. You perhaps just asked yourself, *What voice, do I have an inner voice?*

Her name is gestapo bitch (yes, lower case, she willingly took a demotion, although in the abbreviated form she likes GB). She wears a drab gray color. Her face appears red with intensity and impatience, and her eyes are empty and wretched. She is a part of me. She is not me. She has a role yet has been overworked and under-appreciated and needs way more vacations! Once I befriended her and started to listen tenderly, she revealed a great deal to me. The inner critical voice's prime job is to keep us safe. It is a biological imprint within us to look for safety and avoid threats; gestapo bitch had been on threat alert for too long. I started giving her vacations or simpler jobs to keep her busy. This helped. I know now the more I feel a need to control or feel a life-sucking restriction, GB needs my attention. Once I consciously make these shifts, more joy floods in. Awareness and boundaries are our friends. GB and I are partners in wonder finding.

The women I work with or have sat in circle with for decades have expressed that their inner critic has been in collection mode, hoarding all life's experiences, all outside voices of parents, teachers, clergy, media, and authoritarian figures. A compilation of mass enormous proportions of the unkind kind. We have an inner child voice, often lost and sad, that needs love, and we can call on our inner loving parent voice to provide comfort, to say and do the right thing. It is never too soon to do an internal detox of the hoarded voices and reparent yourself with the love you deserve.

Grace, wonder, and awe found me because
I turned towards them wholeheartedly.
—Lulu Trevena

Messages can come from anywhere; I become the receiver to them moment by moment. The still, quiet, patient energy of knowingness is the Divine's calling and transmission. I feel and know this. It resonates in all things. I continue to lovingly befriend this *voice*. I interchange the word *voice* as it comes both within me and outside of me. It is more than heard: it is felt, it is remembered, it is home. I honor the intimacy and surrender in this presence. This is the place where grace, wonder, and awe are united.

The Tools

Tool 1 ~ The Release

Our bodies have wisdom; we can use them for daily healing. We are more than our brains. Often, stuck emotion, experiences, and energy are stored in our body. We walk around as if we're talking heads and like everything's happening within our intellect. The thinking process has benefits and is limited. We need to connect with our whole body for integrated healing, which supports us moving through any past trauma or wounding, bringing release. Somatic awareness practices are essential.

The Grief Point

There is a point in the middle of your chest that is holding pain.

Once you touch it, you will find the sensitivity there. This point is close to the heart, on the left near your ribs. Locate it with the sensitive touch of one finger. I use my thumb. Our hearts have an immense intelligence and wisdom. In utero, they form before the brain, which shows their potency and importance. When we think, feel, or speak about heartache and heartbreak, we face grief. More than 50 percent of songs are about heartbreak, the price of being human, and all depths of ouch!

When I discovered this grief point through Stephen Levine's work, I transformed many levels of grief. You can too.

Dropping the Armor

There are many ways we have armored, closed down, or built protection around our hearts. We are naturally open-hearted. Unfortunately, throughout our lives and the millions of experiences from birth to today, when we have felt pain, we learned to close off, compartmentalize, and shield vigilantly. Regrettably, we have stored pain in many parts of our body; today, we will work at the level of the heart.

Perhaps you have built a wall around your heart or creatively surrounded it with barbed wire, warding off trespassers. You may have secured it with a padlock and thrown away the key, or it may be wearing armor, clad securely. While it may have felt protected, it is burdened!

Release ~ Dropping the Armor and the Grief Point

This two-step process is dropping the armor and releasing the grief point. This is a daily practice; even in a few days you will notice the grief point is less sore. For your convenience there is a recording resource at the end of this section, which guides you with this tool.

The grief point can be used for any and all grief, not only heartache or heartbreak.

Visually scan or sense your heart, ask yourself *what is around my heart, how have I protected my heart?* Witness and receive. When you clearly see what is around your heart, say to yourself, *thank you for your protection.* Stay with the gratitude for as long as you like, receive this nourishment. Then declare, *I am releasing any and all barriers around my heart now.* Take your time; tenderness in all things. You will notice this will start the releasing process. Visualize all your own vital energy and that of the living light of God and the angelic realms supporting you. Let the armor drop, open the padlock, unravel the barbed wire. Imagine a clang as it hits the floor or thud of the bricks as you dismantle the wall. Use your senses, evoke and imagine; these are powers of grace. See the release and the rubble on the ground. Breathe into your heart, feel the freedom and expansion. Declare, *my heart has wisdom. My heart is safely open.* Breathe.

Bring your awareness now to the grief point. Gently massage it in a circular motion, and push into it. Feel all that pushes back. Feel all that tries to resist, that denies the pain. Let go of the resistance. Let go of the self-protection and declare, *I am releasing all pain and grief. My heart is safe. I am safe*. Do this for seven days straight. It took time to block this pain here; it will need consistent tenderness to heal deeply. These two steps strengthen your self-trust and love. For your convenience here is a recording resource of this section: Recording 1 ~ https://youtu.be/apXHlRBOmmA

Tool 2 ~ Receiving Grace, Wonder, and Awe.

Being open with delight and deliciousness evokes more! Yum, read that again. My wish for you is to approach all that you can with tenderness and embodied presence, especially yourself. Speak and use words that support that also. This tool is a somatic body awareness, which invites you to be present in your body, present to sensations, and use all your senses, all the exquisiteness that makes up our humaneness and delight in having a body. Dear reader, you may want to read this section through thoroughly before continuing. There is a recording resource at the end of this section, where I guide you through this tool.

Grace

Think about your breath. It's automatic.

In essence, you are receiving your breath: just pause for a moment, you are receiving the oxygen that comes into your body and moves through your bloodstream; this life-giving air sending each cell vitality. This happens by itself. You are the receiver of the breath. Gently focus on your breath. There is nothing you need to do. You are the receiver, soften, receive. Receive Grace.

Awe

With your eyes open, I want you to feel the moisture and the warmth within your mouth with your tongue. Let your tongue gently move around your mouth, and then let it come to your lips. There is a gentle delight when you lick your lips with awareness. It is both sensual and brings you to the present moment. It allows your mind to stop thinking. When we are present in the moment, we are not living in the past. We're not jumping forward to the future. Being present in the moment allows for the arising of creative energy, all infinite possibilities, connected to the quantum field. Allow yourself to be so alive with presence that it feels exquisite. Receive Awe.

Wonder

Gently close your eyes. Sense the darkness behind your eyes.

When we close our eyes, we go within, but we can also close down. We often split off from our bodies by default. Stay present; please bring your awareness back to receiving the breath.

Move your awareness to the warmth in your mouth, the moisture, the raw sensation. Now connect deeper in your body by gently squeezing your vaginal muscles. Awareness of breath, mouth and vaginal muscles. Drop deeper. Squeeze gently, with full awareness a couple of times.

Bring your awareness down deeper to your feet, feel them resting against the floor.

Maintain awareness of all these sensations; receiving the breath, receiving the warmth and moisture in your mouth, receiving energy in your sexual organs, and receiving the foundation at your feet. Hold awareness of all areas simultaneously. Breathe. Keep this awareness for as long as you like. Start with three minutes.

Gently raise your awareness up to your eyes and closed eyelids.

Imagine you are a soul artist, and you painted the velvety blackness behind your eyes. Take your time with this. Receive the darkness. Pause here for a minute, you can set a timer, then open your eyes and continue. Slowly with full presence and awareness, open your eyes, allow yourself to receive the light. Receive the images. You are the receiver, your eyes are receiving, not lunging out to see. There is a relationship between the object and your eyes. This is an exquisite process. Receive as if it is the first time you are seeing. Receive with Wonder.

Please use the recording resource for this section, if you desire. Recording 2 ~ https://youtu.be/9wd1fmMKQPk

Your body and heart have wonder to reveal to you; receive them wholeheartedly.
—Lulu Trevena

ABOUT THE AUTHOR
Lulu Trevena ~ Age 59

 Lulu Trevena is passionate about shifting the societal narrative about women and age. Confidence to do anything at any age. She supports women in their own self-empowerment, honoring their personal truth and dreams, clearing what is in the way of embodying their full feminine presence and power unabashedly. Lulu works with a new generation of women who want to lead with their feminine, love their life and body, free from the baggage of the past. Women who desire to fully embody and tap into their inner wisdom from their already rich life and experience, finding their gold within themselves and sharing their gifts to help raise the consciousness of the planet.

She is a Women's Group Facilitator, Workshop Leader, Speaker, Quantum Healing Practitioner, Soulful Living Coach, Art of Feminine Presence® Licensed Teacher, Intuitive Card Reader, Artist, Poet, and Mother. Founder of Live Life with Wonder. She has numerous existing online groups for Soulful Living and Self Expression.

Since childhood, words have held a magical and inexplicable power. Writing has been a sanctuary of wonderment, solace, and salve to her soul. Lulu has been fascinated by the emotions reached by stringing a few words together. Her favorite word is *epiphany*. She also likes to make up her own words occasionally!

Throughout Lulu's message is woven intentional gratitude, deep healing, compassionate soulful living, and valuing each and everyone's journey. Lulu invites us to create conscious forward movement in our own greatness and that we are never too "adult" for a sprinkle of wonder along the way.

You can connect with Lulu at **www.livelifewithwonder.com**

CHAPTER 2

Being Gorgeous

Loving Yourself Right Now

By Kelley Storum, Self Love Course Facilitator, Body Positivity Coach, Love and Touch Therapist

> *"As women in our 50's, I know our struggle with the immense fear of being seen, which is only outweighed by the crushing disappointment of when we are not."*
> —Kelley Storum

My Story

Journeying to gorgeous in my 50's has had me fall in love with myself just the way I am and enabled me to believe I can be the greatest version of myself. My deepest desire is for you to see and feel your body as a temple worth celebrating and delighting in, right here and now, without changing one single thing about you.

It wasn't always this way for me. As a fat kid from a troubled family, shame and discomfort were my closest friends.

At 35, with two small children, a nonexistent marriage, a distant father, and a volatile relationship with my mother, I finally did a yoga class—something I wanted to try for many years. I loved the philosophy but always thought I was too fat.

Meeting my yoga teacher changed my opinions and altered the direction of my life. She was leading a community project and invited me to participate in her Art Exhibition for Women. Even though I jumped at the chance, I was as petrified with fear as I was alive with excitement.

It was January 1999: I remember the evening so vividly. It was opening night at the TAP Gallery in Darlinghurst in Sydney. My little piece was displayed in this big white room filled with as much color and vibrancy as you would see in a luxurious painting. Golds and greens, burgundies and burnt umbers swirling around the room like a complex tapestry - and that was just the people.

The whole gallery was abuzz with fascinating human creatures from all walks of life. The bar area was alive and pumping with deep, intelligent and sophisticated conversation. You could also hear muted mutterings and the mingling of those arty, moody bohemian types (you know the ones). I loved every moment. The atmosphere was vibrant. I was totally in my element but completely out of my comfort zone.

Standing near my little exhibit, I noticed one of those beautiful young arty bohemians walking toward me and heard her say, "How beautiful you are." At first, I had no idea she could be speaking to me, which says a lot about how deep my self-esteem was buried. I tried desperately to appear aloof and interesting. She continued, "I'm an artist, and I'd love it if you would consider modeling for me." At this point, it felt as though my brain had disconnected from my body, and I stood there for what felt like an age, with this gob-smacked, jaw-dropped look on my face, unable to synchronize my tongue and vocal cords. She leaned forward and said, "The only models we ever get are those thin and boney types because they're the only ones that are comfortable taking off their clothes. I would love to draw your curves." *Seriously?* I have no idea how I responded or what happened for the rest of the evening because all I could think about was that conversation. Swirling around in my head was the thought *if I could stand naked in a room full of strangers while they stared into all of my curves, lumps, bumps, and imperfections, drawing parts of me that I had even resisted looking at for the entirety of my life, then I could do anything!*

I never called her.

I did think about it constantly, though, over the next eight years, until I finally did do something. I connected with an online artist's forum and became a life model. It was the most incredibly empowering time of my life. It transformed the way I saw and related to my own body, as well as showing me how unique and beauty-filled we all are.

It was the beginning of my Journey to Gorgeous.

It wasn't that I suddenly became gorgeous - it was discovering that I already was!

My very first life modeling gig was in a quaint little community center for the local Art Society. I could feel my heart trying to burst out through my throat, and I was convinced they could see it, which only made me feel more agitated. I am so grateful, though, to the artists who were so loving and supportive, knowing it was my first time.

In the months leading up to this moment, I made friends with Grant, a Life Model I met in the online art forum. A wonderful, kind, and generous man who took me under his wing and taught me everything I needed to know. *How on earth was I ever going to pull this off?* I had never been comfortable with my body. I was fat-shamed as a child by my family and by kids at school. I believed that everything about my body was different and wrong: my olive skin, my almond-shaped eyes, and of course, my fat!

That night, I was standing in a room with a circle of chairs only a few inches apart and a delusion of creatives, eager to begin their class. All of a sudden, it became apparent the class was filled with men. That situation had never crossed my mind! I felt my entire body curl - not just my toes. I knew there was no way out of this without an embarrassing escape, and that was not an option. Being able to do what I said I was going to do and not let Grant down, my mentor and friend were way too important to me. *I* was too important to me. I was committed to having this breakthrough in the perception of my body so I could be free of shame. I was exhausted from the constant hiding.

The artists were so chirpy and chatty, and it's not like me to have no words, but I couldn't think of anything to say apart from "Hi." One of them stepped forward, "Oh, you must be our model. Lovely to meet you; I'm Edgar. Let me introduce you to everyone." I said, "I'm so nervous. I've never done this before," and Edgar was so great. "I will guide you every step of the way," he said kindly. *Phew! Okay, let's do this.*

Edgar showed me to the change room, where I emerged wearing only a sarong. All eyes were on me.

I wasn't a fat woman or even a woman for that matter, definitely not a wife or a mother. I was a fellow human being making it possible for these artists to enjoy and hone their craft. What I was doing was an act of service to a community of incredible humans who get together every week. They needed me. I don't think they will ever know how much I also needed them.

Edgar directed me into the center of the circle and explained the process. "We will do a few short two and five-minute poses so we can all warm up then we will do a couple of ten-minute poses and have a tea and bathroom break, and then we will come back and do a 20-minute pose, so think about a pose you can hold for 20 minutes." *Whoa! That's a lot to take in*, but Grant had taught me well, and I had been practicing poses in the mirror at home for some time.

It was the posing, the practicing in the mirror, that enabled me to find the courage to model. I learnt that constantly looking at myself naked made it so much easier to be with the fundamentals of who I truly am.

Standing outside the circle as everyone found their seats, I heard those frightening words, "Let's begin," as Edgar motioned with his arm like a model displaying a new car on a TV commercial. His arm swirled by me as I moved into the center of the circle. I took a deep breath, dropped the sarong, and sat immediately on the floor. Why? I didn't think I was physically capable of standing, plus *I'd be too exposed.*

There I was, naked as a newborn, sitting on the floor, posing and being sketched.

It was exhilarating!

Strangely I wasn't even embarrassed. I was a little protective of my nipples and private parts, but to my surprise, the two hours went rather quickly.

I learned so much about what I was capable of.

I was empowered.

While I was practicing my poses in the mirror, leading up to this day, my first gig, I realized my body was just a body. It was big but beautiful. My breasts were not as perky as they once were, but they were vessels of sustenance for my two babies, and for that reason, I loved them. There were slithery stretch lines, silver across my belly which I could reel at in disgust or just appreciate: my skin stretched to nurture the growth of those babies. I could writhe in guilt about too many carb-formed curves, or I could appreciate that I was cuddly and warm and soft.

I soon began to appreciate that I was beauty encapsulated in olive skin with almond eyes and droopy boobs, but I was beauty nonetheless.

If I could feel that way after a life of feeling the opposite, then so can you.

This really is a journey. It won't happen overnight, as they say, but with commitment and integrity, it will happen. The more you practice, the sooner you will see the ridiculousness of feeling loathsome about yourself. It's boring and uneventful and only causes heartache and resentment. It's time to stop.

You see, I know you because I am you. Turning 50 was a major turning point for me as I know it may have been for many of us.

If you're completely sick of yourself, and you are ready to step out of "victim" mode and be the woman you know yourself to be, deep down, the one you protect, then let's talk about Acknowledgement and Language.

The Tool

Acknowledgment

Sit quietly, think, *beauty*. Whatever that means to you. Take some time just for you. I know it feels impossible right now, but you are a Queen, so find your throne for 30 minutes to celebrate you.

Trust me you will want to do this.

First, sit in front of a mirror. Be comfortable, close your eyes and rest your hands in your lap, take five slow, deep breaths and settle into yourself. Hear and feel your breath. Feel your chest rising and falling, and your breath fill your belly. Feel the backs of your legs and buttocks making contact with the chair. Each exhale is as long as or even longer than your inhale.

Can you feel it? That ever so slight sensation? It's peace.

When you're ready, open your eyes. Move closer to the mirror and begin to investigate your face. This is an acknowledgment exercise. This is not about opinions or compliments. It's especially not about criticism.

The meaning of acknowledgment, as stated in the Oxford Dictionary: "acceptance of the truth or existence of something."

Compliment, on the other hand, means "a polite expression of praise or admiration."

Keep this in mind as you draw even closer to the mirror as if to investigate a blemish but this time, just notice. Look into your eyes and notice the differences in color, the size of your pupils, the length of your lashes. Observe the person staring back at you. Look close enough to see the little hairs on your lip and chin. Your ear lobes. Notice your nostrils undulating ever so slightly with each breath you take.

Listen to the opinions of your inner voice, the critic, that often-nasty little voice that points out all of your imperfections. What if those imperfections were what made you, you? What if you could love yourself with and because of all of them?

Now, while looking at yourself in the mirror, investigating all that you see, shuffle back so you can repeat the same process over your entire body.

This time say "I love you" as you pass over each section of your body. Notice the ease or the difficulty in doing so, but do it regardless. You may need to close your eyes at first, or you may need to say "like" instead of love. Be clear; you do not have to feel love or believe it to be true.

Whatever the words you muster, make them meaningful. Feel the vulnerability rumbling in your solar plexus. No one is here, no one can see you, and you never have to tell a living soul what you're doing.

Say it again, "I love you." Say it again. Keep saying it until it resonates. Say it until you can smile, giggle or even laugh at yourself. It will take some time.

If you can get to your toes, well done. For extra bonus points, do it in your underwear. The goal is to be confident doing this naked.

Practice every day. In a notebook or journal, write down three things you can acknowledge yourself for. Start small if it's easier. *I acknowledge myself for waking up before my alarm. For making sure I packed my lunch. For writing in my journal every day for the last week.*

You can graduate to things like. *I have a beautiful smile. I am such a coordinated dresser,* or even *what a great friend I am.*

Next, acknowledge one other person every day. An acknowledgment can land like a compliment for sure. But remember about acknowledgment, the acceptance of the truth or existence of something. An example would be, "thank you, your service is always so gracious." Or "I'm so in awe of your parenting skills" or maybe just "thank you for always being so kind."

Language

Begin to listen more closely to that little voice in your head. Yes, that one. The one we spoke of earlier that insults and degrades you more often than it compliments or encourages. Let's work on transforming that.

The first thing to do is just notice the voice, notice how cruel it can be. Why do we listen to it? We wouldn't speak to our friends, loved ones, or children that way. So why do we speak that way to ourselves?

Then notice the way you speak to others about yourself. At first, just noticing it is enough to draw out its power. You will see how unconsciously we degrade ourselves, and we do it so often that we no longer notice. What are the things you say about you? To yourself and also to others? How can you rephrase them so as not to criticize or condemn?

That little voice will, unfortunately, always be there, but it doesn't have to be so cruel. Following these guidelines, you will become genuinely adept at noticing its severity and, within seconds, be able to ignore it or at least not absorb it as the truth.

Once you've taken on these practices, you will notice new ways of thinking and speaking you've created about who you are and your worthiness.

When you begin to master acknowledging yourself and others, others will begin to acknowledge you in return. Chances are they were always doing it; you just weren't able to receive.

Notice your language when you reply. In the past, you may have deflected any acknowledgment by denying it. This is so invalidating to the person offering it to you.

The best thing you can say, even if you don't believe them or don't want to or maybe just aren't ready to accept it, is just "thank you." That's it. It will eventually sink into your body so you begin to believe it. And most importantly, it leaves the person who delivered it powerfully validated. It's a win-win.

May you enjoy and treasure your Journey to Gorgeous. If you have any questions at all, or you would just love to share the inspiration that has come from your new practices, I would love to hear from you. See my bio for my website and social media accounts.

If you message me from my website I will send you a recording to assist you with the mirror work.

Much love and many blessings xxx

ABOUT THE AUTHOR
Kelley Storum ~ 55

Kelley shares her home with 2 Great Danes and Whippet. Her grown daughters, Tori and Alex, are her best friends and her greatest achievements. Kelley describes herself as a Mother, Lover, vegan, animal and human rights activist, deep thinker, soul searcher, creator of ideas and possibilities, intuitive Massage Therapist, lover of touch, artist, writer, difference maker, and doer of things.

Some say Kelley is often outspoken on things she is passionate about, like injustice and human rights, especially the rights of women.

Learning to love herself has enabled her to give and receive to such a greater depth than ever before.

It is Kelley's dream to create a social enterprise, a sanctuary for women escaping hardship, homelessness, and domestic violence. This sacred space will cater to and house women, their children, and their pets. The rescuing of farm animals will serve to save and rehome them but also teach the women and children how to care for them. There will be offerings of coaching, counseling, creative classes, massage, healing therapies, and ongoing structure and support. A working cafe will be a learning center to train women in hospitality which will enable them to move forward with references for both accommodation as well as work experience.

Finding traditional old-style Lomi Lomi Massage was like stepping into a comfy pair of pink fluffy slippers. It enabled her to experience the importance of touch, invoking all of her intuitive and energy healing capabilities.

Kelley has taken all of her life experiences and now runs online or in-person coaching sessions as well as her signature 14-day live program called BE GORGEOUS. She desires that all women end their negative relationship with themselves and their bodies, remove the shame and learn to love themselves just the way they are so they can be whoever they want to be.

Kelley is on social media supporting and teaching women self-love practices.

Find her at **www.facebook.com/groups/lovetribewomen**

www.facebook.com/kelleystorum

www.instagram.com/journeytogorgeous2

www.journeytogorgeous.com

CHAPTER 3

Life in the Sweet Spot

Five Ways to Let the Goodness Come

By Keren Kilgore, Creative Magician, Quantum Biz & Marketing Coach, Publisher

> ***But listen to me. For one moment***
> ***quit being sad. Hear blessings***
> ***dropping their blossoms around you. God.***
> —Rumi

My Story

The first time I connected with the energy in me it was so powerful I thought I was either being physically elevated or about to have an orgasm. Before this experience, I didn't even know I had that kind of energy. I accessed it within seconds, so it must have been there all the time, buried somewhere deep inside me.

It happened during a witnessed meditation with a group of women. As I stood before them, I was terrified of being seen by anyone, let alone while meditating. But I decided to tap into my courage, jump in, surrender to the flow, and see what would happen.

I closed my eyes and went inside myself. Within seconds, a flow of energy began surging through me, and for three minutes or so, it increased in intensity. Time stopped. I felt like I was transported to another place and was there for a long time. A holy and sacred place where I felt so much expansion in my heart I thought I would explode.

When it was over, I slowly came back into my body and opened my eyes. The women around me stared at me with a stunned look. I'm not sure what they witnessed, but it was so powerful I had to lie on the floor to recover.

I discovered the most precious sweet spot in myself that I didn't even know existed. I felt like I was given the gift of a lifetime!

I have since learned how to access this sweet spot in a moment. I simply *choose* to connect with God. By leaning my body forward (like hugging and receiving) or backward (like resting and receiving) ever so slightly, I can feel a powerful surge of energy flowing through me. Both are powerful surges of connection with the Divine and last as long as I hold the intensity of it. I'm taken into another dimension, where I have open access to my spiritual team. I'm learning to dance longer and longer with the sacred energy within me.

This energy runs deep in every single one of us.

But it wasn't always this way. For more than 55 years, I was disconnected from my body and my own desires. I was always focused on others' needs, even at my own expense. I learned later I'm an Enneagram Type 2 - Helper. Learning to take care of my own needs and even recognizing I *have* desires has been very hard for me. But since finding my sweet spot, pretty much every area of my life has expanded and, as Rumi said, blossomed. Now that I know what a sweet spot looks like, I'm finding them everywhere!

The sweet spots in life are calling to us with every choice we make. They're there waiting to be entered and enjoyed. They don't go anywhere; we do. The sweet spot is never static but is always moving and shifting. We need training to stay in a receptive place and live in the sweet spot.

Life's Sweet Spots

The sweet spot is harmonious balance in just about anything. It's a dance. And it's attainable. Every. Single. Day.

Golfers know the sweet spot where their club hits the ball at the perfect place. If you golf, your hands can feel the connection, and everyone around you can hear it. The ball explodes in the air, and everyone watches with excitement to see where it will land and how far it will roll. You know it the moment you hit that sweet spot. And when you know what you're capable of, it keeps you playing.

A tennis racket has a very defined sweet spot right in the middle of the strings. There are racket sleeves to train you to only hit the ball in that center three-by-three-inch space. And when you hit the ball and feel the power of it leaving your racket, you know you've done it right. As you prepare for your next shot, you watch the ball land just where it was intended. And you can feel your heart expand with the feeling that comes with being in the sweet spot.

In baseball, the sweet spot is the point on the bat where contact with the ball doesn't cause the bat to vibrate. All the energy goes into the ball, causing it to soar.

In relationships, it's about the dance. The sweet spot is found where the desires of one person overlap with the desires of another. Because desires shift, so does the sweet spot, so we're in a continual dance with our partner to explore and stay in the shifting sweet spot. It requires intuition, our senses, and movement. If we're not participating in the dance, life just isn't as sweet. I can't count the times I've misconnected in a relationship and felt the painful vibration of missing the sweet spot. It motivated me to learn and grow with every encounter.

Parents know when they've hit a sweet spot. Their young kids can shower by themselves, get dressed, and maybe even do a decent job wiping their own butts. As a mom, I remember the feeling when I told my son to go take a shower and him coming back with wet hair and clean jammies on. I felt like I accomplished something significant as a parent.

Even plants have a sweet spot. When a palm tree is planted in just the right place, it continually puts out long shoots of growth that eventually open into great big palm leaves. It loves doing its job of being a good palm tree.

We all have a job to do, and when we do it from our sweet spot, it is so much easier and so much more fun.

Finding Our Sweet Spot

The Japanese Ikaigi symbol diagrams the sweet spot beautifully (go to **www.quantumshiftmedia.com/www-book** for a downloadable PDF of this symbol). It's our reason for being or getting up in the morning. When we find the sweet spot between vocation, mission, profession, and passion, we find the most joy and sense of well-being. This is where we light up and feel our life has meaning, value, and impact. When we're just off-center, where the vibrations are painful, we feel stuck. This includes feeling satisfied but useless, comfortable but empty, excited but uncertain, or delighted but enjoying little profit.

When we're in our sweet spot, the vibrations are so pleasant and powerful they can carry us to another realm. That's where the dance is the sweetest. I experienced this the first time in witnessed meditation.

A mangrove tree sends out seedlings or propagules that look like a stick and are ready to grow apart from the tree. The propagules can drift for weeks or even months. They look dead but dance in the water until they start to grow roots that weigh them down until they are floating vertically. They eventually snag onto something, such as an oyster bed or rocks.

From there, the propagules grow more roots that dig deep into the sand. That snag was the baby mangrove's sweet spot, which enabled one root to give live birth to an entire grove of trees. The mangrove's root system is a nursery for all kinds of sea life and the entire grove is so strong it can cut the power of a hurricane's damage to land by half. It can take a while, but when a mangrove finds its sweet spot, everything in nature benefits.

According to Wikipedia, a sweet spot is *any place or set of conditions that is optimal for obtaining a certain desirable effect or result.* For the mangrove, it was snagging an oyster. For a baseball player, it's the center of the bat. For a mom, it's when the kids can make their own PBJ sandwich. For the entrepreneur, it's when they have addressed the places they are stuck and their life and business are in optimal balance and in alignment that they can soar.

When we find our sacred calling in life, our Ikaigi, we find optimal balance. It moves and shifts, and we have to dance to stay in sync with it, but it expands us, and we can tap into its power any moment. We know when we've hit the sweet spot in sex, in our routines, in meditation, in our health, in parenting, in relationships, and in our life's work.

What does that sweet spot feel like to you? For me, it makes me smile. It lights me up and fills me with deep gratitude. I find it when I'm water coloring. Or walking in a park and touching a tree or feeling the breeze on my face. Once you recognize them, sweet spots show up everywhere!

What would it take to live in the sweet spot all the time?

The Tool

5 Tools to Keep You In Your Sweet Spot

1. *Using Frankincense Essential Oil and Saying the Mantra: Let the Goodness Come.* Essential oils are not only potent but carry powerful energy. Frankincense is the king of oils. Among its many beneficial properties is strengthening memory. I've survived eight traumatic brain injuries with no long-term damage, but anything I can do to send love to my brain is welcome.

Try this practice every morning. Rub a drop of frankincense oil on the crown of your head. Raise your arms in the air and say out loud, "May all the goodness come to me and flow through me today. I welcome it and receive it."

What you focus on expands. This practice sets your intention for the day and sets the stage for continual connections with the sweet spots. When you are in alignment, you can feel the surge of energy run through you. Take a few moments until you feel the warmth of gratitude expand your heart, then get ready to receive whatever is coming in your day.

2. *Practicing Meditation.* It's an active contemplation, not passive reflection, that gets me in the sweet spot of meditation. It's making a conscious choice to connect day after day that increases your capacity to handle more energetic wattage. How much would your wattage capacity increase if you stopped three times each day and tapped into your Source?

One time I was meditating and the question, "Where is my safe place?" popped in my head. I realized my safe place is right in the middle of my spiritual team. I was immediately taken up into another realm and found myself in the middle of the Trinity. They were three individuals and one whole at the same time. I stood right in the middle of them and felt their energy surging around me like a whirlwind in an infinity shape. I was invited there and given free access to them any time I wanted. Since my first witnessed meditation, I learned how to contain the ever-increasing power surges. I know what a quantum shift feels like, and I was in it. I knew I was having an out-of-body experience.

I often say I will hold space for someone. As I stood in the middle of the Trinity's surging energy, I showed them my cupped hands like I was showing them something I was keeping safe. They all looked in my hands and saw the people I was holding space for there. Then, with what felt like a snap of their fingers, they put into action on a cosmic level what was needed in each situation, and things began to shift in the universe.

I'm now able to go to this most precious place many times each day. What makes my joy-meter soar is not only the energy I feel but the opportunity to take people with me and hold space for them in the presence of God. What would make me even happier is to lead others to this place. The door to it is a solid meditation practice. You can use whatever meditation practice lights you up. Your spiritual team speak many languages.

What works for me is aligning my vertical core—head, heart, pelvis—and feeling the energy from the earth surging from my feet all the way through the top of my head. It can start at the top or the bottom and surges up and down in waves. I feel connected and can feel energy from the earth and the heavens surging through me. I can feel my heart space expand with the amount of energy running through it. Sometimes, I can feel my throat expanding. Other times, I can feel my mind or belly space opening up. It's a tangible connection with energy.

The more I practice being in this space, the longer it lasts. Sometimes, all I do is close my eyes and I'm in the energetic flow. If I lean slightly forward or backward, I can feel it even stronger. As I practice meditation, I'm getting better at hitting my sweet spot.

3. *Choosing Creativity and Pleasure.* As Feng Shui experts will tell you, your space is important. Feng Shui means wind-water and uses energy to

bring harmony between you and your space. I have a wonderful place to work. My studio is full of the things I love. LED fairy lights hang on the ceiling. I have a sit/stand desk, two chairs in front of a gas fireplace, a triangle-shaped art table with watercolor supplies ready, a workout area with weights, a stationary bicycle, a guest room, and a private bath. Out the sliding glass doors, I have an outdoor office with a table next to a pond where I work most of the spring and summer. Something very expansive happens when I swing, so I hung two hammock chairs where I can sit and meditate or get a download of insight or creativity. I put two chairs next to the two swings, so I can meet with clients or have friends and neighbors over, and we can all enjoy the sweet spot. I love this space. I made conscious decisions on each element to experience as much pleasure as possible, and the amount of creative flow that comes to me in this space is remarkable.

Your space makes room for creativity. Make your space a happy place. For me, spending even 15 minutes painting a watercolor lights me up. I believe *everyone* is artistic. If you have put any limitations on yourself that you're not, you've robbed yourself of valuable sweet spots. Art doesn't have to be perfection; it simply needs to light you up.

What do you want? What would make you a little more comfortable or make something a little more fun? Is it sitting in a particular chair or pulling a footstool over to prop your feet on? As you read this, what big or small thing can you do to create more pleasure? Set your intentions and feel into them.

4. *Getting Outside.* There is something special about being outside. You can feel the energetic connection of being in the sweet spot when you are hiking a trail. Seeing the intricacy of a flower can be glorious. Stop and put your arms out and soak in the energy of the sun on your skin. Take

a moment to tune into the sound of a river running over rocks and feel the sweet spot.

I was at the beach with my family recently and watched an osprey dive into the ocean, grab a fish with its feet, and soar overhead, circling and then landing in its nest to feed her young. I couldn't stop watching it. My heart soared right along with her. Those moments are sweet spots, so stop and enjoy the energy they carry; it will expand your capacity for more. Sweet spots happen all the time; we just need to notice.

5. *Receiving From my Spiritual Team.* I have a successful coaching business that launches entrepreneurs. With the amount of flow that comes through my company, I've learned to rely on my spiritual team for wisdom and direction and use this tool to distinguish our responsibilities.

To create your spiritual team chart, draw a line down the middle of a piece of paper. On the left column, write *My Responsibility,* and on the right column, write *My Spiritual Team's Responsibility.* Write down all the things you need to do in the left column. Then write down all the things your spiritual team should do in the right column. For instance, I need to write a blog. That goes in my column. In my Spiritual Team's column is *inspiration and ideas for the blog.* In my column is *follow up with Sonja about her website.* In my Spiritual Team's column is *insight to know what Sonja is struggling with right now.* When you're done, you may feel release and freedom surge over you just knowing that your Spiritual Team is going to carry their responsibilities so you don't have to. Find the sweet spot in that dance because your list is ever-changing.

May you find your sweet spot in every area of your life. May it give you confidence, creativity, and courage. May it light you up and ignite the flame that burns within you. May it be the catalyst to impact the world through everything you say, everything you do, and most importantly, who you are.

ABOUT THE AUTHOR
Keren Kilgore ~ 64

Keren Kilgore works with gifted visionary leaders, authors, and entrepreneurs who are stuck when it comes to promoting themselves. She creates a quantum shift by turning ideas into practical strategies and creative messaging so that business owners can attract their tribe and make an impact. Her coaching focuses on communication and marketing, strategic branding, websites that rock, and publishing to get books out of people's heads and into print.

Energized by creativity, Keren loves hiking canyons in Colorado, filling her laundry room wall with Monet-like watercolor art from her four grandkids, cooking a gourmet meal with friends, playing Canasta, and enjoying a scotch on the back porch by the fire with Michael, her beloved husband of 40 years.

A lifetime book lover, Keren has ghostwritten, edited and published hundreds of books for authors in numerous genres. She is currently writing a book entitled *Can I Call You Mom?* about her 26 teenage foster kids and what they taught her, a children's book entitled *Blink,* and has begun a mystery novel.

What lights her up is helping business owners through radical transformation using creativity, courage, intuitive wisdom, and group communication. She loves working with entrepreneurs in their second career who have a real passion and vision to change the world and want to leave a legacy. She empowers them with the tools they need to get launched.

Keren can be reached at **QuantumShiftMedia.com**.

CHAPTER 4

When Death Comes

Finding Peace in the Face of Unimaginable Pain

By Yantra-ji, Therapist, Artist, Author, Educator, and Spiritual Teacher

Shattered – we don't want to hear, or feel,
another death another shock
the mind reels, how can it be, not here not now
But death is love's own handmaiden,
shock and devastation the doorway
We deny that we are called to enter, hurting,
humbled at the feet of love
Love will take us one by one, until we reside at home
We are asked to trust this love, this breaking heart,
these dripping tears,
and shaking limbs, those howling sounds
It's love's voice, love's hand, clawing us back to her bosom
Through your sudden departure, which leaves us weeping,
shattered, speechless
No longer fighting, we can surrender here,
discover together beloved
you and we are loved and free

—Yantra-ji

When death comes, not *if* but *when*. By age 50, we will have experienced many deaths: death of our childhood, of innocence; death of our ideas, dreams and hopes, projects or careers. We may experience the death of our youthfulness, health and vitality, death of our childbearing body as we move through menopause, death of relationships, as well as the death of the physical body of those we know and love through trauma, accident, injury, suicide, and illness.

Even though most of us fear death, all of these changes we call '*death*' are not bad. They may be unexpected, painful, and unimaginable, but ultimately if we are willing, they lead us to living a life fully aligned in love, peace, joy, and freedom.

Death comes in so many guises. What all of these seemingly different deaths have in common is the pain of change: changing form, changing circumstances, changing our relationship, to who or what was, will no longer be, and to what actually is.

While we know death and change are inevitable, we still try to deny that death will occur. Along with this denial comes added pain and suffering as we try to avoid the unimaginable pain of any change, loss, death, or trauma – ultimately, we avoid the gift of love.

There is a way we can be broken open by love—if we are willing—and receive love's gift even when it's not wrapped the way we expect.

It is my hope in sharing a tiny portion of my life's journey with death, along with simple and often overlooked tools we all have access to, that you may find peace, freedom, and hope in the face of any unimaginable pain that you will inevitably encounter.

My Story

I was no stranger to death. It called me to be strong for others, while inside, I was filled with fear, dread, panic, and suffering. We like to be prepared, but nothing can really prepare us for death or unimaginable loss.

My first daughter was 11 months old; I'd woken to the phone ringing, shaken from a dream. It was the police. No details were given over the phone, but I knew by what they were not saying. I could hardly stand, hardly breathe. The accident; I was dreaming it as it had occurred. The police came. Within the shock, I was internally screaming *no, it couldn't be true, I'd just seen him a few weeks before, just spoken to him that night on the phone, it must have been a mistake, not her dad but someone else in the car.*

It was a long drive from Sydney to Forster to meet his parents, then to Kempsey to the police station morgue; my mum was with me and my baby girl and his stepdad. As I stood terrified, hardly able to breathe, hoping, they slid back a little window. There was no preparation for what I was seeing, *no, no, no,* my mind was screaming *it couldn't be him,* but it was. They'd combed his hair and beard; he didn't look like he should; he was dead. I felt dead, crying for hours on the trip home, in shock, numb, through the funeral, through that next year.

I had grief support, counseling, alternative therapies; then a switch flipped as though suddenly I was back here, as though I'd awoken from a dream, a nightmare. It had taken a lot of healing to find myself again, and even though I felt like I was a new me, I had a new relationship, a new life, the pain of grief and loss was still present.

A year later, I was asked by one of my dearest friends to attend the birth of her third child. When I was called to the hospital to be by her side, it was too early. I could feel my own fear and hers. Taking a deep breath and shrugging it aside, I went. I didn't like hospitals, but there I was, holding her hand, dealing with the doctors speaking to me, as she was not quite with it, having been given strong meds for the physical pain. The doctor was shaking his head as he mouthed the words to me, "the baby has no heartbeat; it's got to be delivered now." My eyes were wide with the horror of it. I was crying inside, *no, this can't be happening, delivered now, her baby will be dead.* I turned back to the bed, my eyes locked with hers.

I could only hold her through my presence and gaze as she delivered her little girl, tiny, un-breathing, lifeless. She was unable to move due to the birthing and meds, and with a pleading look was only just able to ask me, "please look at her, tell me what she looks like, I need to know, please before they take her away." It was shocking to be asked, shocking to have to look, and shocking to have to tell her, but my love for her was stronger than my fear.

It was hard. There was no time to think about it. I had to be quick before they whisked her dead baby away. I was both shaking in shock and calm, the calm taking over to do this inevitable, beautiful, painful thing. I said, "she is beautiful." I couldn't say *she is pink, turning blue and grey,* the words swirling through my mind. I couldn't say, *but she's dead.* I couldn't say, *no, I can't, don't ask me to, I'm horrified.* Devastated, with panic rising, just the words "she is beautiful, perfect, so tiny, she looks just like..." And yes, she was. I went home, still numb, others expecting me to be as I was, life as normal, no understanding of the depth of what I'd just experienced, and no one to share it with. Even as I write this, the edges of panic want to rise, and so I open and breathe right here and now, as I share this with you.

A friend and I were sitting in a park. He'd self-harmed but said he was now okay; he was getting help. He didn't tell me he had a mental illness or was on medication or that there were other times. I never knew till later, when his father spoke with me, and then the police. Instead, we sat in the park, on the grass in the sun, warming our skin, and talked and talked until he knew that I knew he was okay. It was the last time we spoke, the last time I saw him.

I left disturbed by our conversation but feeling he was okay, or so I thought, until the call came, saying that he'd died. They said it was his illness and that he hadn't expected to die, but he did. He'd gone too far. I felt the burden, the weight, as though I was somehow responsible. As though I should have been able to stop it, even though I couldn't have known. Even with all the help he was receiving, nothing could have changed it.

There were many more deaths to come: family friends, close friends, cancer, accidents, then my dad, colleagues, later my own divorce (another type of death), and still more deaths. As I write this, a friend is taking his last few days with loved ones, and another dear friend has just passed suddenly, unexpectedly. The poem I started with was for her.

Through it all, I was growing in maturity, wisdom, understanding, spiritual insight. I had many tools and gifts, but it was still painful, often seeing these events in meditations or dreams before they happened.

I worked as a practitioner in alternative therapies, seeing clients and running retreats. Then in Steiner Education with children, parents, and mentoring others. When my work came full circle back to becoming a Journey Method Practitioner in 2002; I was facilitating other practitioners through their training, again working with children, parents, seeing clients, and running retreats. Through the Journey Method as a healing modality, so much had changed, so much healing, opening, and letting go. I learned to open, to meet whatever was arising, any thought, sensation, pain, or emotion; to forgive, to be complete. I felt free, unburdened, but still, nothing can prepare you for what is to come.

It was a different death this time: the pain of betrayal, the truth surfacing, death of a relationship, of family, a divorce. It took everything to stay present, true, and open in the face of so many lies, so much deceit, seeing my children being used, and in pain. I felt the pain emotionally and physically, the tragedy of it all. The only thing I could do was to stay true to my deepest prayer *to be true to the truth, no matter what*. And so, I kept opening: being willing to stop, right here, to pause, to breathe, to be still.

It was like standing in the face of a raging storm, waves crashing against me again and again, while I was breaking apart, breaking open. With each unrelenting wave of deceit, each wave of fear, each wave of hatred, anger, despair, it drove me deeper and deeper into this vast ocean of presence, through forgiveness, understanding, acceptance, awareness, into the stillness, silence, and love that remained untouched. Unexpectedly I remained at peace; deep inner peace through it all. This peace remained, and *no matter what came*, I was free.

Fast forward to January 1, 2012. It seemed the best possible start to a new year. I felt so open, free, and clear. Life was good, really good. Then the unexpected came, change came, devastating news, and again all I could do was keep opening. Then when I thought it couldn't get any worse, a mother's worst nightmare: my teenage son unexpectedly died.

I was heading to spend the day with another spiritual teacher. My son was at his dad's house, which I had to drive past on my way, and I had a feeling of foreboding. Something was wrong. In the middle of that day I felt a shattering inside me; so did my littlest daughter. As we drove home there were unusual detour signs along the way. I was fighting an unexplainable urge to go against those signs, to go down those roads as each sign arose.

When we got home, that knock at the door, the police. I already knew it was my son. They wouldn't tell me where, but I knew that too. I'd seen that accident, felt it in my body a few weeks before, not knowing at the time it would be him. Again, I was internally yelling *no, no, no*, and out loud, "it must be a mistake," but I knew. My legs were weak; I was in shock; devastation, unimaginable pain. It was another unraveling. It was as though I was both fully present, aware and feeling it all, and separate from my body. There was more to come, to be uncovered through his death: the police, coroners, questions, was it suicide, funeral, ashes, and traveling back to India. And through it all, through this unimaginable devastating pain, there was peace.

To say it was unbearable, painful, and devastating cannot describe the heartbreak experienced. Even though we can never be prepared, on some level, I was. In my willingness to stay present, to not move, to meet the waves of pain, disbelief, the shock upon shock, through the crashing of each wave, there was undeniable peace and profound love.

When I say there is nothing too big to handle, too intense to meet, this is the truth. When we are willing to be broken open by love, by all of the different faces of love, we discover we are truly, endlessly, free.

When my dad was diagnosed with cancer, I thought those early experiences with death had been preparing me for his death. They gave me strategies for 'coping,' but none of it prepared me for the pain and loss I might experience when he died, nor for any of the subsequent deaths, including my son, and this, of course, is true for any death.

We grow in wisdom and life experience, but nothing can prepare us for a moment we have not yet experienced. Our minds would have us believe we can be prepared. Ultimately nothing can.

Yet how we do one thing is how we do everything. This means how we are with life is how we are with every change, including death.

Nothing can ultimately prepare us for any change, death, or any unexpected or unimaginable pain. But the good news is this: to the degree we are willing to be fully with life, our spiritual habits muscle is strengthened, which allows us to open to experience the peace that remains even through death.

The Tool

Are we willing to meet the pain of death, loss, and change?

Is our heart able to bear the unbearable? Are we willing to be broken open by love? Can we really discover true peace, love, joy, and freedom, no matter what?

I would not usually refer to a tool or technique. Rather I would point us to who we are. It is who we discover ourselves to be that alters our whole relationship with what we have believed to be ourselves and our experiences of life and death.

So how do we do this?

Each moment is an opportunity for us to open or close, to be present or in denial, to suffer or be at peace.

It starts with our willingness to ask a simple, truthful, and profound question:

What do I want? Deeper than all of the superficial wants and desires, what do I want? And if all of that was fulfilled, what would that give me?

This question of inquiry directs us to see truthfully, deeply, what we most want.

You see, we might say we want truth, peace, love, or freedom. But, only if it looks like this, only if it means I get to that, not if it means this or that!

This inquiry question has us face deeply and truly what we want. We may discover we want to be loved, seen, respected, safe, or in control more than we want peace, truth, or freedom. Truth-telling is so important.

I wanted to be true no matter what, free no matter what, and so life as it does, tested my resolve: What about now? What about here? What about in this situation or circumstance? Again and again, I said *yes to truth, to God, to grace, to life, to love, no matter what.* Then, the ultimate test: My marriage ending and my son dying; to stay true, still, present, aware, free, and at peace, even in unimaginable pain.

Again, how we are with every moment of our life is how we are with every change and every death.

It's our willingness to be here and now, not wishing for anything to be other than it is, that allows peace. As each thought of wishing, any story of past, future, what was, is, or will be, all the "what ifs" and "if onlys" create pain on top of pain.

As an Exercise:

Right now, just pause, take a breath, notice fully this moment. You are holding the book; your eyes see the words. As you breathe, you notice the sounds outside, the sounds inside, notice sensations of your skin, in your body, emotions, and thoughts. Whatever you notice, let it be as it is.

You don't need to like or dislike it or change it. If you notice you are telling a story about what is here, just stop, pause, breathe, open. There is something deeper, quieter, still, silent, aware, and at peace, regardless of the experience of body, mind, or emotions. Let yourself open here, right now, to the discovery of this silent grace. This is who you are: free, whole, unaffected, silent, at peace.

What usually happens is we have a glimpse of the truth, then pick up the identity—the story of me and my life—and wonder why we are suffering. Then the true invitation comes, a test of our willingness to not move, to not follow a thought, a sensation, a story of past, or of future. And this glimpse is what has our whole attention. We find this glimpse then is our whole life; it is who we are.

Life, death and pain occurs as it does, and we are free. For ongoing support, please see About the Author Yantra-ji and Living Alignment.

Silent reflection
Let your heart be moved
Your mind be silenced
Your breath be as it is
The heart beating its rhythm
Of life's love
Of life's loss
Of life's joy
Of life's pain
Silent reflection
Let the time pass as needed
Your life be slowed
Your attention here
The moment calling you
Meeting all that arises and falls
As life and love
As life and loss
As life and joy
As life and pain
Silent reflection - gratitude
—Yantra-ji

ABOUT THE AUTHOR
Yantra-ji and Living Alignment ~ Age 55

A renowned therapist, artist, author, educator, and spiritual teacher, Yantra-ji offers insight and transformation through self-inquiry.

Originally born in England, immigrating to Australia as a young child, she grew up in Sydney. Through her early 20s, she searched for a deeper spiritual connection in life, working with health, wellness, self-development, spiritual practices, the creative arts, and Rudolf Steiner Education. At 55, she is a mother of four, stepmother of two, and grandmother of seven.

A deeper realization occurred through the meeting of several spiritual teachers, which opened the possibility of this grace that is always here.

A profound awakening came from the introduction to Sri H.W.L. Poonja, affectionately known as Papaji. His simple message, "to stop, to call off the search, you are already free here now," had a profound effect on her life.

Yantra-ji's commitment is supporting and confirming the realization of the truth of who you are – regardless of gender, form, identity, life, or circumstances – that you are free here and now.

A therapist for 30 years, offering meetings in truth, Satsang, self-inquiry, and the Founder of Living Alignment, the embrace of support for this direct discovery into the truth of who we are. Author of *The Gift of This - Poetry and Prose of Satsang with Yantra-ji*; *The Fire of Grace - Staying True to This - Satsangs with Yantra-ji*; *Profound Awakening – Meeting Papaji Now* and soon to be published *Spiritual Habits – Incremental Moments Leading to Lasting Freedom*, all available on Amazon.

Information on in-person and online meetings, private consultations, therapy sessions, and retreats can be found on the website and Facebook pages. Free guided meditations and videos are available as support on the website, Facebook and YouTube.

Living Alignment Website: **www.LivingAlignment.com**

Living Alignment Facebook:
https://www.facebook.com/LivingAlignment

Yantra-ji and Living Alignment YouTube:
https://www.bit.ly/Yantra-ji-YouTube

CHAPTER 5

A Conscious Closet

Your Vehicle to Transformation and Empowerment

By Daniela Caine, CPC, ELI-MP, CTDS, Coach and Designer

"How we do anything is how we do everything."
—iPEC foundation principle

My Story

It was about to be my time to go up on stage. I didn't feel great, I came down with something earlier in the week, but I felt good enough to present thanks to the cold meds. I chose a woolen jacquard cape to wrap myself in, almost like a Wonder Woman blanket that made me feel both strong and protected. Clasping my script, I calmed my breathing down, got off my chair, and walked towards the stage.

My friend and boss for this project, Kim, introduced me to the crowd of salespeople who filled the ample event space. Over the years, they saw a revolving door of designers with different viewpoints circling through the company, making them understandably apprehensive of yet another new perspective and direction.

"When I accepted the job to become VP for Womenswear here at Pendleton, I knew I needed a talented and passionate designer to help make this brand pivot possible. My first phone call was to Daniela, and I am so glad she said yes!" Kim explained. "I'm letting her talk you through some of the fundamentals we put in place before presenting the items in the collection."

I braced myself, got up on stage, found my spot behind the podium, unrolled my manuscript.

Inhale. Exhale. Focus. I looked up.

"Good morning, everyone!" I beamed.

"It's hard for me to put into words how much it means to be here with you today. The fact that I am presenting the FA/HO 18 collection is a dream come true. I used to tell everyone who would want to listen—or not—how much I believe in this brand and its potential." I chuckled a bit; it was the truth.

"Before we dive into the details of the collection, I wanted to talk a little bit about the design ethos and the design filters we established to help ensure that each piece of clothing we designed is meaningful to the brand. One of the most important questions we asked ourselves with every garment, no matter how basic: How will this make the wearer feel?"

"I strongly believe that clothing holds energy. Our clothes can make us feel empowered, beautiful, comfortable, sporty, and so many other ways. With each garment in this collection, we wanted the wearer to feel empowered, strong, and beautiful."

I became more comfortable, seeking out eye contact with the audience. Now they were engaged, their body language relaxed, some leaned forward in their seats.

After the introductory part, my merchandising counterpart took the stage to guide the audience through all the garments in detail. The design team took turns in presenting the monthly themes. After five hours of presentations, the unimaginable happened: The crowd got up on their feet and gave a standing ovation.

I looked around; everyone on the team was beaming from ear to ear. The merchandising director even had tears in her eyes.

We had done it!

I was exhausted and happy when the day came to a close. Looking for Kim, I walked down the narrow dark corridor to her office.

"I just wanted to come by, say thank you again, and wish you a good holiday break before I head out," I said.

"What an amazing day, right? It was the most challenging project we've ever done together, and the most rewarding one too!" she replied.

"That's true," I responded. "It might sound strange, but after so many years doing this job, it feels like I've finally arrived! Thank you for giving me this opportunity." My eyes welled up.

"I couldn't have done any of this without you." She said. "Next year, we'll talk next steps, okay? The CEO already mentioned that he'd like us to take the lead on the other categories. Maybe you can start thinking about accepting a full-time position?"

"Sounds amazing, Kim! Yes, let's talk next year!" I responded.

"Have a great winter break." She smiled with outstretched arms.

We gave each other a rare hug before I walked back to my desk, got my bag, and called it a day.

A month later, my world fell apart.

Our ten-year-old daughter, Leona, started to feel unwell around mid-January. By the end of the month, she was bedridden. Week after week, we saw doctors, but nobody knew what ailed her. At first, I tried to hold it all together, straddle work and a sick child. In late March, I sat down in Kim's office, unable to hold back tears, and told her I wouldn't be able to finish the current collection. Something was wrong with Leona. Whatever she had, I had to figure out what it was and then hopefully fix it.

It took until late May before a blood test finally gave us answers: Her celiac numbers were through the roof.

"She may have celiac disease or be very gluten intolerant." the pediatrician said. "I'll give you a referral to a GI specialist."

Unfortunately, the pediatric specialist had a way to communicate with children that left me furious, and Leona traumatized and terrified of doctors for years to come. When we finally found a doctor who included alternative healing methods, her fears eased, and we got tangible help.

It was pretty easy to pivot our food choices, but we had no idea how long it would take Leona's system to eliminate any gluten remnants. She had missed half a year in school, but we were determined to get her back on track over the summer break.

By the new school year, she'd be thriving and caught up with the curriculum, I imagined. *Maybe I could think about going back to work?*

All looked promising until the school year started. Each morning, on the way to school, Leona would crouch over with stomach pain. Her face pale, forehead scrunched, tears in her eyes. She was in agony.

Maybe she needed more time to heal?

It went like that for days and weeks. After a month, I started to get desperate. My dreams of getting back to any sort of normalcy, of working again drifted away.

"Not in school again?" My husband called incredulously.

"Nope. Couldn't do it. We'll try again in a few hours, maybe. When she feels better." My typical answer.

Some days I drove her to school three times without success. Some days, she was able to stay for a couple of hours; if she was at school, I often got called to pick her up early.

School wasn't the only area of struggle. Leona panicked at the thought of being left alone at home, even for just 10 minutes. Grocery shopping made her spiral into anxiety attacks. Driving over bridges or through tunnels made her feel dizzy. She hated being in a car. All the things that once brought her joy—singing, ballet, gymnastics—now seemed impossible. My once social butterfly became a terrified recluse.

I felt I had no right to complain, though. I was lucky I didn't have to work. I didn't want to burden my husband with my frustration and desperation. Leona was the one who suffered the most, and her condition was challenging for him too! He already took care of us financially, and I saw it as my duty to take care of the rest.

After yet another failed attempt at drop-off, I hit rock bottom.

All the anger, pain, and frustration, all the emotions I bottled up for months, were finally boiling over. I marched from the school building towards the adjacent highway and screamed my frustration into the cars flitting by. My throat now hoarse, I grabbed Leona's shaking hand, walked back, got in the car, and called a therapist.

I needed help.

After this episode, the principal stepped in, ordered my husband to start doing drop-offs, and politely asked me to stay away from campus. If Leona was allowed to call a parent, it had to be him from now on.

"I'm sorry to say, but you are a trigger." The school nurse said.

I was devastated. I failed even at being a mother?! I had totally lost control.

I started going to the therapist and finally allowed myself to talk about all I had lost, the guilt and shame of being incapable of helping my daughter, my inability to fix the situation, and how useless and worthless I felt.

In retrospect, I know this was the breakdown of my identity. The scaffolding of my ego had collapsed. Slowly I realized how much pressure I was putting myself under!

I started meditating and enrolled in a coaching program. My mother flew in to help with the family while I went to a weeklong meditation workshop in town. What I experienced during that week changed me forever.

I was able to experience energy on a physical level that I didn't know existed. At one point, I felt it flowing through me in wave-like formations, moving my body in ways that defy my conscious abilities. In one of the meditations, I felt my heart opening up so far and wide, sensing it way beyond my physical body, and I wondered: *How is this even possible?*

After three days, I realized there was more to life than what meets the eye. I was joyful, in love with life for no reason other than being! For the first time in my life, I sensed that my worthiness was not related to being a successful or productive member of society. For the first time in years, I felt grateful for everything that had happened. It led me to this underground conference room in the Marriott Downtown Portland, where I found myself sobbing, in awe and wonder, after experiencing a transcendental awakening event in a deep state of meditation.

A whole new, exciting world started to open up for me.

I meditated daily and dove deep into the coaching program. I had no idea what I was doing but decided to trust the process. Throughout the training, I got coached and coached others with terrific results. Like a sponge, I absorbed everything I could learn about energy, spiritual practices, meditation, coaching, epigenetics, and quantum physics.

Over the following years, major shifts happened for our family. The more I let go of control or my need to fix, the better Leona became. The more I healed and learned about myself, the less pressure she felt, which allowed her body and mind to relax. While turmoil unfolded during the pandemic in 2020, our family cocooned and surrendered. Leona healed. I coached and offered workshops online and continued learning and expanding, curious to find my place of impact in the world.

I lived in the question: *How could I utilize and integrate everything life had gifted me?*

My friend Danielle, who is a talented material director and shares an interest in meditation and spirituality, dropped a big clue one day:

"Did you know that materials have energetic frequencies?" Danielle asked during one of our conversations.

"What? Seriously? I never heard of that!" She got me hooked.

"Yes! I just had this interview and presented this to his team."

"Kanye West? Seriously? How did they react?" I asked curiously.

"Didn't say much. His people said they'd get back to me," she said.

"I'm blown away by this, Danielle!" I said, wondering if Kanye would understand it.

But I was electrified. This was it! A missing puzzle piece!

I always knew clothes had energy. I used to design thinking about how the wearer would feel! Yet, it never occurred to me that fabrics have energy. *Does the sewing operator influence the energy of a garment? Would the love and care of an artisan positively impact the frequency of a garment?* A deep burning and too-long-buried desire re-emerged: I always dreamed of launching a brand. Now I couldn't wait to start playing with those new ideas, energy, frequency, and of course, it would be grounded in ethical and sustainable manufacturing.

I started interviewing women, friends, and colleagues, using my new coaching skills and, became curious about women's thoughts and beliefs around clothing. What I discovered blew my mind: There were so many stories about clothes, both empowering and disempowering. I realized the more conscious the woman was—no matter if it was spiritually, environmentally, or ethically—the more difficult it was for her to truly desire anything. Whatever she bought ended up being a compromise with a pinch of guilt sprinkled on top.

"The designer handbag and my spirituality don't match," one woman said.

"I feel so guilty supporting corporations that exploit the people who make the clothes. It's okay to shop for my kids, but I hate shopping for myself," another underscored.

"I primarily buy second hand because I feel guilty buying anything new given the impact those clothes have on the environment," added a fellow designer.

Women less concerned about the environment were caught in a hamster wheel of consumerism, constantly looking for the next trend but too often left never feeling satisfied. Some ended up regretting their purchases, stuffing them deep into drawers to never wear them.

Statistics around our clothing consumption are staggering. Did you know that the average American woman only wears 20% of the clothes in her closet? And of the 32 billion garments produced each year, 64% are thrown away unworn or after just one single use?

For all women, fashion was a guilty pleasure, a vanity, indulgence, superficial. But we all enjoy the idea of wearing something that would genuinely make us look and feel good. Of course, we do! Our clothes are our second skin; it's how we communicate nonverbally who we are.

It is so unfortunate and no surprise that so many of us have disempowering thoughts about clothes in general. I wondered, *what if we all felt empowered and happy with what we wear? What if the daily ritual of getting dressed could be a source of joy and good vibes?*

That's when I realized that our inner blocks, those pesky voices in our minds that keep us right in our comfort zone, show up in our closets! What if we used our wardrobe to become conscious about our own limiting beliefs? How fun and playful, and yet so profoundly insightful would that be?

I became curious about my own stories about clothes and how those beliefs showed up in my closet. Were the clothes I owned empowering or disempowering? I realized that my own closet felt stuffed, messy, overwhelming, and disjointed. I realized I often waited for things to go on sale before I purchased anything. I didn't go for the clothes I actually wanted and often went with a compromise.

Why? Where else in my life did I limit myself? Why did I believe I didn't deserve what I wanted in the first place?

Many of the clothes I owned were from brands I worked for. In my industry, we express brand loyalty by buying and wearing the clothes we produce, so having a good selection of branded clothes was an unspoken rule. I always got employee pricing, which caused me to buy more than I really wanted.

Where else was I trying to fit in and sacrifice? Or where else was I loyal in ways that didn't really serve me?

And of course, the good old pattern: hanging on to clothes that didn't fit anymore, hoping that one day I would lose the weight and be able to wear those jeans again. *Wasn't this a daily reminder of my 'failure?' Not exactly a sign of kindness towards myself.*

I became obsessed with the idea of building a wardrobe I truly love, where everything I pick makes me feel fabulous, which would automatically raise my energy and outlook for the day. I imagine each item representing who I am and who I want to be, and all of them aligned with my values of sustainability and ethics. *No more compromises,* I promised myself!

The Tool

Now it's your turn for discovery. Let's get those hidden inner blocks to come out of the closet!

Imagine you are in your closet or in front of your wardrobe. In your mind's eye, picture your clothes, the colors, fabrications, prints. Is everything neat and in order, or are your drawers overflowing? Are clothes on the floor or piled up on a chair?

Do you feel expansive, joyful, free? Or do you feel heavy, condensed, or even overwhelmed?

Just sit with the energy, let it be what it wants to be. There is no need to fix anything. Just notice what's happening in your body.

Now, in your mind's eye, focus on your clothes. Where does your attention go first? Do you see color? Texture? Individual items? Your favorite jeans or the elegant suit? Is it exciting, or is there monotony? What stands out for you?

Do you have a uniform you rely on but feel like you are in a bit of a rut? *Where else are you not stretching and growing? Where else are you stuck in your comfort zone?*

Do you have a wardrobe full of clothes but nothing to wear? *Where else do you take on too much that weighs you down or doesn't serve?*

Is your wardrobe full of stuff that doesn't fit? Either the wrong size or simply not representative of who you are or want to be? Are you hanging on to clothes you paid a lot of money for? *Where else in life do you have difficulty letting go?*

Do you believe you can't afford more expensive clothes or the quality you would like? *Where else in life do you think you are not worthy?*

Are you afraid you might get unwanted attention? Are you worried about being judged, judged for being vain, a diva, too self-important, too beautiful, too powerful? *Where else do you dim your light not to upset others?*

Do you simply not care about your clothes and appearance because there are so many bigger problems in this world?

Where else do you spend all your energy worrying about others, desperate, maybe even angry about the state of our world?

Take out your journal and jot down your experience. What blocks did you encounter? Where was the most energy?

Now just a few quick tips and easy guidelines for building your conscious closet:

Think about who you want to be and how you want to dress. Create a mood or Pinterest board with anything that inspires you.

Give yourself permission to be her.

Seek out the best quality you can afford.

Buy mostly natural fibers - they have the highest frequencies.

And most importantly: Buy what you love.

If you prefer to enjoy this tool as a guided meditation, come and visit me at **https://www.danielacaine.com/resources** to download the audio recording as well as the closet inventory spreadsheet I created to become super conscious about my own wardrobe.

ABOUT THE AUTHOR
Daniela Caine ~ 48

Daniela Caine is a Purpose & Core Energy Leadership coach and a designer on a mission to empower women and girls across the globe. She brings 20 years of global industry experience, having worked for brands such as Nike, Pendleton, and Adidas, and wants to use her background to help change how women relate to the clothes we wear. She believes that when fashion is conscious, it's not vain or a guilty pleasure but an act of love. Her clothing line, Koryphae, launches in late 2021. Sign up to learn more and become a founding member at **www. koryphae.com**

CHAPTER 6

Healing is a Love Affair

The Path, The Truth, The Life

By Ghislaine Bouskila, CEMP, Kinesiologist, Breathworker, Workshop Facilitator

"The greatest gift we can give humanity is our commitment to constantly raise our level of consciousness and vibration."
—Ghislaine Bouskila

My Story

"Michel! I have Lyme disease! Can you believe this? Finally, I have an answer. I now know what it is that I have been suffering from for so long!"

"Lyme disease? Wow! Are you okay?" It's still a bit early for him. I waited as long as I could to call him, but this time difference business between Paris and Sydney is unmanageable today. I urgently needed to talk to my husband, regardless of the time zones separating us.

"I'm so happy I came to Paris to use this lab. You should see what else they found in my blood sample!"

A person suffering from Lyme disease will have other bacterial, fungal, or mold infections, worms, parasites, viruses, and heavy metal toxicity, making it difficult for the detoxification process.

"I knew my symptoms were not in my head!" I continued in a high-pitched voice, "I knew it wasn't depression or Chronic Fatigue Syndrome or whatever else the doctors wanted to diagnose me with. I knew there was something else! I knew it! I'm so happy I understand now; I feel so relieved!"

The medical establishment often misdiagnoses Lyme Disease as there is no adequate testing available, and the range of symptoms experienced is wide. Many are being treated as psychiatric patients.

Lyme disease, named from a town, Old Lyme in Connecticut, USA, is transmitted through the bite of a tick which carries the bacteria Borrelia Burgdoferi from the name of the biologist who first recognized the bacterium. Lyme has now been identified in many parts of the globe, and different species have been listed. Borreliosis is more frequent than one thinks, as it is hard to diagnose. Bioenergetic blood analysis is best adapted to get a reliable result.

"This is big!" Michel doesn't know how to take the news. The last few months, I kind of knew this was the reason for my irrational symptoms. Immense fatigue, debilitating migraines, frightening hair loss, sharp electrical-like discharge in my body, stiff neck, sore throat, strenuous menopausal symptoms, loss of words, coughing fits, and excessive sweating at night had kept me unable to go on with my days.

"Yes, this is big! I'm scared! I'm feeling all over the place!"

"When are you coming home?"

"I don't know yet. It's crazy; I'm feeling elated and terrorized at the same time. I feel I have been avenged by the results, which is great, but now I have a big task, understanding how to deal with this! At least I have a sense of direction, and I like that."

Practicing kinesiology, breathwork, and a variety of energy healing modalities equipped me to make progress in dealing with my symptoms. I was on the road to recovery using the path less traveled since my first child's birth 30 years ago. At age 17, I suffered from Crohn's disease. Moving to Australia eased the symptoms. I went into remission, or so I thought until my body experienced the stress of giving birth.

"If you want to stay in Paris, take your time. Why don't you enjoy your family a bit longer? Tell your clients you're taking a bit of time off."

I sit down, take a breath.

"Yes, I could do with a bit of time off," I answer absent-mindedly, wiping tears off my face.

"You've had a difficult year. The truth is you've not been able to keep up with your timetable. You've had to cancel many days of work because you couldn't get out of bed. Don't you think…" he started to say.

"…it's time to stop," I interrupt him. "Yes, I know it is. You're right. Since the Breathwork Conference I organized last year, I haven't been able to recuperate. It feels like the floor is constantly giving way from under my feet. I need to find my bearings."

Stress may be physical/environmental or mental/emotional, suppressing the immune system allowing for invisible enemies to invade the body's ability to regain homeostasis.

"This sounds like a good idea!" I can hear the triumphant smile of my dear husband of 33 years.

"I love you, speak soon," I have no strength to go further on this conversation.

I remain on the couch. A torrent of tears floods my being, jerks my body. I allow myself to drown.

I could be dying from this! My days are numbered! My life as I knew it will never be the same! After all those years of healing myself, I can't believe there is still enough negativity in my body for this crap to thrive! What is escaping me?

Why is my body going from one disease to another? I really need to increase my immune system so it can fight this naturally! Something has got to change!

This is an opportunity for you to go deeper Ghislaine! Something is missing, and you know it! Time is up! You need to make the most of your life!

The Tool

I knew I wouldn't go the modern medicine way. My previous experiences had sufficed to show me that chronic symptoms need to be addressed on the physical, mental, emotional and spiritual levels, all at once.

On the physical level, I support my immune system with orthomolecular, herbal, and homeopathic medicine, clearing and cleansing my body with what the earth has to offer.

On the mental level, I slow down my over-activated nervous system by grounding myself. I make peace with time. I come out of survival by reassessing all thinking which makes me believe that I am not enough, that I need to do more or try harder.

On the emotional level, I welcome my emotions without fear. I sit with grief, sadness, or despair. I connect with my inner child. I give her a voice through creative endeavors. I decide to no longer betray myself to please others.

On the spiritual level, I release control, and I let love heal me.

I use the gentle healing power of the breath to heal my cells, connect to my truth, and gain the courage and confidence to live a creative life.

I share with you my grounding breathing meditation.

Use it unsparingly when you feel your nervous system has been over-activated and you can't focus or rest.

Use it when you feel urgency, panic, confusion, grief, anger, blame, or total exhaustion.

Use it when you need to feel held and loved.

Sit in a comfortable chair with your feet touching the floor. Make sure you will not be disturbed. Put a nice, beautiful, soothing, and relaxing playlist in the background.

Connect with your breathing, just observing what it's doing. Relax. Increase the inhale in your lower belly, in your navel area. Put your hands on your navel to make sure your breathing is emerging there. Let your belly rise when you breathe in and go back down when you breathe out.

Start your session with breathing in and out of your nose. If your nose gets blocked, breathe in and out of your mouth. In conscious connected breathing, the emphasis is on the inhale; the exhale is totally relaxed.

Connect your inhale with your exhale and vice versa. There is no pause, no breath retention. Your breathing aligns with the rhythm of the waves in the ocean.

Connecting your breathing is how you will calm your nervous system. Feelings, emotions, and thoughts will emerge, develop, and integrate.

The physical sensations in your body might increase, diminish, move to another place, or disappear. Stay with whatever is happening in your body! Breathe into it, relax into it.

You might get an image or a memory in your mind's eye. Observe and connect. Is there anything you need right now, in the picture, in the memory? What would you need to feel good about yourself, about your life?

Refrain from "psychologizing" the answer. Stay open to what will come up, if and when it does. Let go and allow yourself to be surprised by the answer.

Enjoy being outside of time, of purpose.

Enjoy being in breath, connected, and conscious.

Bring your attention to your feet, connect and breathe. If you find it difficult to feel your feet, squeeze your toes a few times.

You are now connecting with the earth, with Mother Earth. Start drawing on her beautiful, grounded, and warm energy. Pull up her energy on your inhale.

Let her nourish you. She knows you. She knows what you need. Feel her warmth, allow it to gather in your lower body, at the base of your spine, in your belly, nourishing you, relaxing you, enlivening you. To gather more energy, you can squeeze your perineum muscle a few times.

Enjoying the relationship you have now created with the earth, receive her in your heart. Receive on the inhale and give on the exhale. What you are craving for is exactly what she needs. Give her tenderness, love, compassion. Let her know she is precious to you.

Your breath now reaches your third eye, located in your forehead, between your eyebrows. This is the seat of the pineal gland, your metaphysical connection between the physical and spiritual world. Breathe light, breathe awareness, and breathe love ever so gently, softly. Bring a smile on your lips, relax the muscles of your face; you are now connecting with the heavens.

Receive ease, certainty, and support from the invisible world, which looks after you and guides you endlessly. You have a legion of angels, guardian angels, and spiritual guides looking after you. They maneuver on your behalf for your highest good. They open the way, they protect us, and they guide us, always! Ask them to inspire you!

Ask your ancestors. Their desire is to assist you in healing the trauma from past generations. Feel them: they gather in a messy line, striving to be in front so they can be the one supporting and helping you. They might not all be wise, but they all usher positive energy towards you. Ask them!

Stay there, connecting the earth with the heavens, through your body, and through your breath. Let your breath do the breathing. Receive the gentle healing power of the breath. No efforts. Just relaxing into being.

Stay there, feeling taken care of, knowing that life will take extremely good care of you. Learn to trust your life. Accept. Forgive. Love. Know there are no mistakes. Relax, enjoy your journey. There is no rush; it's all planned. Learn to receive. The earth and the heavens want to give you their love, light, and creativity. Take it!

Stay there in this peaceful, nurturing, and enlivening relationship until your eyes feel like they want to open naturally.

Write, draw, sing, dance, walk in nature, become who you are.

Breathing in this full, conscious, connected way gets you in touch with your inner teacher. It connects you with the all that is within and without.

Chronic diseases result from a feeling of separation and disconnection from the loving and nurturing energy of the Universe.

One of the most damaging ensuing separations is the one we have from ourselves, from who we really are, our original nature, and from our ability to receive universal love.

Separation inevitably happens at birth, and the trauma most of us experience gets repeated during our early developmental years and throughout different life experiences. To survive the traumatic experience, we establish a belief system based on fear, hurt, or confusion. Our breathing pattern becomes impaired while suppressing emotions and feelings. This leaves an imprint on our nervous system, on our physiology, and psychology.

With each separation, there is a thought. Our thoughts are creative; they have an impact on our health.

With each separation, we let go of a part of ourselves. Our ability to love and receive love is compromised.

With each separation, we lose the connection with who we are. Our life enjoyment is diminished; we lose direction and focus.

Breathing consciously heals your mind to create peace, heals your body to connect with your truth, heals your spirit to feel presence, and heals your soul to live in grace.

"Now is the time, and love is the way."
This sentence, from James Twyman's book, *Emissary of Love, the Psychic Children Speak to the World*, (ISBN1-57174-323-5), has stayed with me since the moment I read it early on in my studies. It has defined the way I worked. I have used it on my website, in my blogs, and as a constant reminder of the power of love in healing. I would always come back to that truth each time, with each crisis and with each healing.

Environmental factors contribute to disease, but our over-activated nervous system prevents the immune system from functioning optimally.

Our autonomic nervous system gets aroused when we feel insecure and dependent on what feels outside of our control. To gain our togetherness back, we need to learn how to be there for ourselves, lovingly.

We need to sit and welcome the thoughts, emotions, and feelings that are unpleasant. We need to learn to slow down to be with our wounded self, giving it space, time, and tenderness.

The truth lives in our bodies. Our body shows us the way. Our illnesses, accidents, and losses are there to remind us to realign with our truth. It's so easy to get lost! Our body never lies; it doesn't know how to. If we listen, it will show us the way to a better life. When the mind gets involved, the words of our story will get louder than the whisper of our heart. And the heart will have to wait to liberate us with its light and its love.

Frank Ansell, a traditional Indigenous healer of the Nungkari Tradition, with whom I spent time in the Eastern Arrernte desert country in Central Australia, suggested I repeat every morning:

"Heal my Mind; Heal my Body; Heal my Spirit; Heal my Soul"
I did it for many years, repeating this prayer three times a day. It took me a while to really get that my suffering lives in my mind and my mind only. I know now I can heal my mind with the love of my heart.

Love is the most powerful energy we have to change and transform what the mind perceives as wrong, bad, or ridiculous. Your heart is your connection to your real self. Your emotions are the messenger of your soul.

Listen, follow, and acknowledge your emotions. They are valid. They are important. You need to honor them. They will lead you to your truth. Pay special attention to your grief. It needs your love, and in turn, it will open the door to your inner beauty.

Gently mother yourself, the child in you will wake up. If she has been hiding in fear, shame, or guilt, she will now feel safe to be who she is. Embrace her, love her. Make her feel important. Stand strong for her dreams. Give her your voice!

There is no other purpose to your life than learning to love yourself so that you show up and make a difference. There is no other purpose to your life than to increase your vibration so that you can light the world with your smile. The gentle feminine aspect of tenderness, receptivity, creativity, and transformation is so powerful, and it's yours to activate daily. It's only when we love and accept ourselves that we can love and accept others genuinely. Love is not an insipid energy, and love is not subordinate to someone else's approval. Loving ourselves fully will right co-dependent relationships and all relationships based on needs. Those keep us afraid, attached, and out of integrity. It takes a while to know who we truly are.

It's a constant work in progress. It's a gentle daily self-inquiry to align to the integrity of our original nature.

We are here to create love. When we do, we unite the earth with the heavens. We heal the planet! What else are we here to do? It is not an easy project, this self-love adventure. Isn't it the reason why we are here?

I now say yes to my life every day. I welcome and accept whatever it brings me. I don't need to control it because I know that the love that lives in my heart will take care of me. I have learned to welcome my emotions without judging them. I am not afraid of being sad; I sit with it. I know that underneath the grief lies my divine self. When I feel disappointed or angry, I know what I need is more love. I learned to sit and inundate myself with love. Love needs no reason other than this is our natural state.

I healed my relationship with time, and I am at peace with my rhythm.

I understand everything is movement. There will be good in the bad and bad in the good. It's the perfection of life, and it promotes my evolution. I surrendered to the love of the Universe. I allow myself to be loved and to love. I anchor myself in my heart every day!

I am here to play!

ABOUT THE AUTHOR
Ghislaine Bouskila ~ 59

 Ghislaine's personal experience in healing herself from chronic diseases such as Lyme disease and Crohn's disease, plus her 20+ years of clinical practice has led her to develop her Conscious Energy Medicine program using Kinesiology, Breathwork, Energy Medicine and Spiritual Psychology.

Ghislaine loves using a gentle approach to healing as she understands the nervous system and how it functions plays an important part in the vitality, creativity, and well-being of a person.

She understands that the healing of the heart and that the fulfillment of human destiny is influenced by the events of life and our interpretations of them by the mind.

Ghislaine is the Australian National Representative for the International Breathwork Foundation (IBF)

She holds a diploma in Breathwork Mastery and a Diploma in Kinesiology.

She has been dedicating her professional life to sharing the gentle yet powerful healing power of the Conscious Connected Breathing process through one-on-one online sessions, group sessions, her blogs, and her participation in various local and international conferences.

To connect with Ghislaine visit her at

Website: **https://www.consciousenergymedicine.com**

Facebook: **https://www.facebook.com/consciousenergymedicine**

Instagram: **https://www.instagram.com/conscious_energy_medicine/**

LinkedIn: **https://www.linkedin.com/in/ghislaine-bouskila-1ba25520**

You can sign up to receive her monthly blog:
https://www.consciousenergymedicine.com/blog

To experience a breathwork session:
World Breathing Day 2019 "Breathing into Grounding"
https://www.youtube.com/watch?v=RqV9FAR_Gn8

To hear more on grief: The Good Grief conversation with Janet Jones on UK health radio
https://www.ukhealthradio.com/player/?ep=21919

To listen about children: The One-Year school podcast with Barbara Hoi, on children **https://podcasts.apple.com/au/podcast/pc-13-ghislaine-bouskila-kinesiologist-breath-worker/id1529979254?i=1000500121948**

CHAPTER 7

Wise Woman Goes WOW

A Juicy Approach to Invite Wonder and Live a Miraculous Life

By Mi Straznicky, Artist, Visionary Leader

"Where the mind goes, the energy follows."
—Ancient Chinese quote

My Story

"I feel numb. Totally numb. I'm not feeling anymore. I'm like a zombie, just functioning. No life, no love. Neither receiving it nor giving. I even have to remind myself to eat and drink. There's just this paralyzing fatigue. My body is so exhausted, struggling with various dangerous issues. And the worst? This is all causing me to get fat. All those years of working too much, over-functioning, being continually stressed, and hardly sleeping are now taking their toll on me. Totally overwhelmed, I frightened everyone away or actively outpaced them, as I did with all my love affairs and admirers. I'm finished with love anyway. Can't be there for anybody anymore." I muttered all of this into the massage bed while my ortho-bionomist, dear friend, and coach was reordering my bones. "Now I'm lonely. And you know what, I'll be one of these middle-aged women, the never-having-a-man-in-her-life-again type, a little artsy and showing up in loud dresses (more tents than anything else) and trying to hide her sparse, white hair by tinting it, and wearing extravagant jewelry."

It wasn't true that I didn't feel anything. I did feel the tightness of my muscles, each muscle individually, weighing tons. *They're pulling me down; I'm pure lead.* Talking about all that was lacking, I felt them tightening even more. *Drama-mode, yeiii.* Each area my friend was working on felt as if hot arrows were shot into my flesh, traveling up to my brain, and breaking through my head. *Interesting!* I almost enjoyed it, as it was at least something I felt. I could focus all my pain on this torture and blame her.

"Excuse me, but this doesn't sound like you at all." Her voice interrupted my new plan to be a victim. "Forget everything you've been taught about aging. That's nonsense. Just be who you are and stop assessing it. Normally it's you coming up with a story of what could be good about it or why it's not necessarily what it seems to be. Or you're telling me something about being wise but never old."

I should have known better—her words, all sharp knives, triggering worse than her work on my physical trigger points. "I do not want to think positive," I grumbled. "There is no story left for anyone. I just want to hide and live a quiet, happy life."

"I'll give you a month with that," she laughed. "You are a great soul, and great souls want to take responsibilities. You have always been inspiring others, and you will feel the call again. Just give yourself the time to heal. We are allowed to be anything. Even weak and deeply sad. Sure, you're exhausted. Could you please honor yourself for all you've been doing, and thank your body for doing it all with you and letting you know in its language, that loving attention is needed, would you?"

"You know I don't believe in the separation between the body and me, nor the body-spirit-and-soul-thing. We need to reconnect what never was separate. We are just we, in one part," I declared defiantly, knowing the same moment that I was talking myself into troubles. *Bye, small life!* Shame and some anger were setting a kettle on fire and flushing my cheeks with the steam that needed to spread in my body. She got me caught in her net.

But over the years, I've learned to forgive myself for not being perfect, wise, or authentic in every moment and to accept help in those moments I'm not. "Thank you," I sighed and immediately felt less stressed. Even my jaw became soft. "Obviously, I got entangled by life. I'm terribly lost. Only a month ago my mom died all of a sudden, and now my children are on their way to conquer their own lives. It feels like someone pulled the rug out from under my feet. And all the walls and shelters with it. The coating layer above is gone, and the base fades away. Me in the middle, fighting to keep the balance, flailing my arms vainly in my attempt not to fall into the abyss. Last Friday night, I found myself sitting alone at home with ice cream and TV, thinking, *this is it now. This is my future.* If there had been any energy left, I would have felt betrayed by life in general and my newbie adults in particular, who come home to steal all my loving attention, get lunch served, empty the fridge, leave some washing, a minimum of six water glasses, and half-emptied, sticky cereal-bowls in every possible place, just to disappear in the evening. Gone into their exciting new lives full of parties and fresh love, from which they had torn me out with their naked existing."

"So true! You should write a book," she giggled. "Look, it's okay to feel upside down. And also, that you won't let yourself feel right now. You had quite a hard time. It would be too much pain to bear. You protect yourself with this numbness. I can understand. You need to sleep, get well again, and grieve. You need to feel miserable and don't want to change a lot right now. But what about adding something good and beautiful for you here and there?"

I was always a fan of the organic flow of inviting what you want.

She continued, "About the loneliness, you are such a sensuous woman. Creative and always full of passion and ideas. People feel you are connected to a bigger reality and with all beings. Did you know that some friends are calling you the elf? It's about you talking to stones and your contagious love for joyful living with all your senses. You are known for the huge variety of spices and full drawers of ingredients to mix cosmetics in your kitchen. And think of your paintings. With your special way of accepting everyone as they are and your alternative stories of unpleasant situations, you make people feel good in your company. And I heard being invited to one of your parties can turn life into something magical. And the most important: I've never seen you without love in your heart. It's your super-super-power. Find your way back; there's no need for any effort to help others, just be and share that all!"

"Sensuous, huh? Sharing who I am, yes?" I left, cocooned in my thoughts. *Shit!* My stomach curled up into a knot; I felt my cover blown. I kept myself invisible as much as I could. I was raised in the strict belief that the best way to survive was not to draw attention to yourself and the worst thing that could happen is to be seen. Trying to be "normal," I was hiding for decades. I pushed down the call for something bigger. My family were the masters of invisibility. They had to be. Past times weren't for folk, highly intuitive, gifted, siding with those who can't talk for themselves and with a passionate sense of justice. Quite a challenge for a tall girl with a passion for wearing colorful patterns, opulent styles, and glitter, paired with a zeal for art and performing. It was always working against me—Hard work, no gratitude. Fighting down big parts of me was what kept me working harder than anyone else in my job and overly caring for family and friends, and it was what brought me to the edge of my well-being. I supported others to become themselves, to avoid becoming myself. My favorite sabotage act was getting really big as an excuse to hide and wear boring clothes and have an extra layer of protection against everything. Yet a voice inside me kept yearning for something else. *I can't relate to the elf nonsense.* Feeling the fresh air on my hot cheeks walking back home after this intense session, I am fully aware that this kind of judging myself will not help anymore. *I'll be good to me from now on. The war is over. Survival mode, back to the medieval, true self, activated, check. I finally confess: I am magic.*

On this day, I became my true self again. Better and unstoppable.

This could be it. The big turning point. My recipe for everlasting fidelity. The truth is it was not. I'm more the spiraling type.

I already knew most of that before. I just like to ignore it in dark hours like these—no exciting turning point. But I picked out the *adding something beautiful* and created a program to invite wonder. This is exciting. Thank you, Katharina!

So, I'm meandering towards the goal of being fully me. It's a journey with alternating ups and downs, hiding and excavating, pushing down parts of me to be like others, feeling disconnected, pulling them out again, and so on. But you know what? No big breakthrough is the big breakthrough. A constantly circular movement to develop, that's how it works for me: nothing special, but all extraordinary.

And I'm a collector—a collector of impressions. I grow by watching and breathing in atmosphere like a whale would sip the whole ocean and gather the tiniest bits to nourish the biggest creature. That's me sucking in situations, words, and examples to digest them in my universe. What fits or enriches me gets integrated, or something new is built from it. Something wonderful.

Wise we are, anyway. You can't get to 50, or any age, without collecting knowledge and expertise and a tremendous number of strategies to make life work better. But where is the WOW? Is it fun?

I've seen so many wise women offering advice and help, being a role model for alignment, independence, and sobriety. We try to prove old beliefs wrong by not being able to be classified, sexy, empowered at any age or brave *fempreneurs*. Do we always wholeheartedly enjoy it? Do you think wisdom is the final station? I tend to say it's more a natural step. Sometimes I'm missing the creating-with-relish-part, the spark. In my opinion, we all have forgotten that we are true creators. We have unlearned to *sparkle*. Wanna try?

What if us **being** is already the miracle? What if the answer is **lightness** instead of seriously becoming enlightened? What if being **joyful** is wise? Life is hard, they told us. How do I activate lightness? How to regain the spark?

To find out, I gave myself permission to be everything, in every moment. As long as I choose it, yet I can choose to ignore it as well. Or to be dull or cruel or brilliant or caring or super lazy or denying all my gifts, and hide under the most comforting blanket. Or use all of these feelings or tendencies to inspire. Or choose not to. This is always a way, too. It's all in me. The important thing is not to attach to the outcome, not to judge.

Be the creator of your life! My choice was learning by doing and by trial and error. And what errors! I celebrated black waves of self-consciousness. I bathed in the feeling when life seems to have blown a big hole into your midst, and you need to constantly wrap your arms around yourself, trying to stabilize the rim of the crater. I loved, so strong and unrequited that even breathing was a sharp pain cutting through my lungs, and I had to force myself to inhale and exhale. Later, I buried every feeling so as to never suffer again until this burial was more suffering than any pain could cause.

I just decided to live all of life with joy. There is no prohibition to enjoy intense feelings.

And no limitation to what you want to experience. Life is a story, the one you write!

But I'm convinced as soon as you fully step into being a creator, you'd rather glory in creating fascinating, beautiful things more than anything else.

The Tool

Too spooky for a start? Here is a 5-steps-gateway tool to further your experience:

Open up for the possibility that you are wrong. Things may always be different than you think. The forward-pressing 'idiot' in the car behind you may have his birth-giving wife on board.

Open up for joy. Brainstorm what makes you happy and marvel. It may be different from what you think. The number 1004, for example, always makes me smile—no idea why.

Open up for miracles. Start with looking for them once a week.

Open up for indulging in magical moments in your daily routine.

Invite wonder into your life by recognizing it's already there.

For a demonstration, I'd like to invite you into my universe. Ready? Take a big breath, and here we go. If you were Mi, you would have chosen a rainy morning for a walk, enjoying the tickling raindrops on your skin. You look for pretty things in the shop windows. Only a few passengers hurry down the street to escape the weather. Maybe there is a traffic jam or some honking cars.

Did you hear? One has got a tune instead. Like a cellular memory of India with its liveliness and chaos and all honks tuning differently in the shadow of the ancient temple you are visiting, with your mouth full of honey-sweet holy cakes and a jasmine necklace enfolding you with its mesmerizing scent. You can nearly smell this amazing fragrance in the street walking by a couple kissing in the rain.

Hey! You see a little flower growing between the road-stones. It's so beautiful with delicate petals and an enchanting color. Maybe you can smell its sweet scent, like your honey-cakes before. Along the street, you notice more plants growing brave into the grey.

Oh! And there is a bumblebee! Can you see it? If you stand still for a second, you can hear its cheerful humming and see the furry thing diligently visiting the prettiest flowers. A sunbeam could find its way through the fluffy rainclouds straight onto your face.

Mmmhh, it feels so good, and believe it or not, there is a little twinkling fairy riding the bumblebee buzzing into the sun! She waves at you and wishes you a good day. You may be a little puzzled, but I guess there is a grin on your face, growing into a big smile. A stranger walks by. Your smiling eyes are meeting theirs, and their face begins to melt into a smile as well for a precious moment of connection. Looking back over your shoulder, you notice that this scene is repeated with the next person the smiling stranger meets. This exchange is all initiated by your infectious smile. You can envision how the second person is smiling at another, or even two strangers, and how it's spreading the magic to another hundred people or more. Done. Made the world a little better today.

You arrive at home already good-humored. You can't help but jingle the bunch of tiny silver bells hanging on your entrance door. Such a delightful sound! You choose not to scream immediately because of the thousands of different shoes spread over the entrance floor. Maybe the fairy flies by later and clears them up?

After successfully fishing the fresh bread out of your embroidered shopping bag, the bag itself threatens to fall off the counter. "Later Mizzie. Sit! Be a good girl!" As you directly bite into the crunchy loaf, you breathe in the heart-warming smell. Maybe you have also bought a puffy *pain au chocolate*, which you adore for the soft, sweet pastry hugging the richness of the chocolate inside, sensuously melting its delicious bitter and sweet on your tongue. A symphony of sensations. You definitely need a coffee with it. Or a tea? The coffee-lover in you prepares it today with added cardamom and a hint of cinnamon. Or the tea specialist decides this is a day for some elegant Darjeeling with rosebuds. Or maybe you change your mind and have some milk, an almond drink, or water.

Just be playful and add what comes in handy and feels indulgent. In any case, let the scents and taste transport you to exotic places full of adventures and magical impressions. Ha! This calls for gathering all your cushions and arranging them on your sofa. Oh, and somewhere is some Turkish delight left that somebody brought as a present once. On beautiful dishes, you serve all that for your majesty, the mysterious queen of your kingdom. Dressing up is optional.

The advanced version of you would grab a piece of fabric and fasten it on the walls above like a baldachin. The little girl in you, instead, might demand a castle made from umbrellas, ropes, and other oddments. Just give your "rationalist" self the day off.

"Thank you, Mizzie!" Satiated like this, you find your shopping bag still well-behaved waiting for you. *That music again*! The neighbors or your kids? They clearly must be training for some underwater event! That's why they need to turn the music so loud that they can hear it with their heads stuck under water in a bucket.

The herbs on the windowsill are moving in the wind, and their little dance is spreading new scents of pleasure into your kitchen. "Actually, that's a good idea," you compliment them and let yourself get taken away by the rhythms, dancing your shopping into shelves, fridge, and baskets. And the shoes into the closet. Just before heading towards the rest of your wonderful day at work.

I am magical, and so are you. Explore the magic for yourself.

For the guided meditation and free 7-days challenge click here: **https:// lightnet.exchange/resources**

Mi Straznicky ~ 51

Mi Straznicky is an artist, visionary leader, relaxation coach, Qi Gong trainer, practitioner of Access BARS, PMR and Ra Sheba, and a wedding planner for passion; works as head of the finance department for WAG Assistenzgenossenschaft.

She is the founder of lightnet.exchange, a platform for ex/change, reinventing future, awakening, art, and world-changing projects. Mi deeply believes that the biggest problems are to be solved with the simplest tools and by the smallest unit – each one of us.

Currently, she is working on the concepts for the movements 'revolution of the smile' and 'pandemic love.'

In her work, she is passionate about awakening people's true self and about environmentally sustainable and mindful corporate reorientation. Her goal is to lead individuals to achieve their biggest dreams with lightness and joy and live on their own authority. She will always stand up for the birthright for glitter as she is contagiously spreading sparkle.

Willingly she shares insights to her Cosmos, and Visions. Come to meet her on the personal site linked to her platform.

When not at work, you can find her in the kitchen dancing while cooking either indulgent desserts or cosmetics, pampering her indoor jungle, or in the sun at some water. Mi ecstatically loves her family and friends, calculation and fishes.

e-mail: **mi@lightnet.exchange**

site: **https://lightnet.exchange**

fb: **https://www.facebook.com/facemiwork**

instagram: **https://www.instagram.com/mistraznicky**

CHAPTER 8

Mine the Lessons of Your Life

Uncover Hidden Joy

By Joy Resor, Spiritual Mentor, Minister, Joy-Bringer

"...The more closely we can listen to our soul's desire, and follow its call, the more clear our paths in life become..."
—Elizabeth Gilbert

My Story

Every now and then, how much I love life overwhelms my being.

After decades feeling I don't belong, struggling, and hiding, I'm grateful to be fully embodied, open-hearted, and awake to the mystery living through me.

May these tales inspire you to embrace, honor, and love your life, or to heal, grow, and change so you can.

Seeds of Separation

When I'm three weeks old, we move to Loring Air Force Base in north-eastern Maine. Toddler sis is active all day while newborn me tunes out her shenanigans. I'm awake all night. Exhaustion overtakes Mom, so Dad finds a crib for me in the base hospital.

Growing up, big sis picks up words Dad utters as a joke, repeatedly sassing this litany at me:

"Mom and Dad put you back in the hospital because you cried too much. Then they got the wrong baby back. You **really** don't belong in our family!"

The painful words swirl inside me on repeat for years. I don't belong. I feel separate from my family, and everywhere I wander.

I wait alone until Mom picks me up late from Brownies, band, and track. Big sis slams the door in my face when I want to talk and sneaks nasty letters into my locker. Braces, glasses, and orthopedic shoes. I wear a bright dress to the dance among girls twirling in sherbet hues. Friends drink beer together. I swim laps alone. With an internalized sense of not belonging, the world always reflects this back to me.

What do we do when feelings can't be expressed? How do we connect when we must be silent while the news airs during dinner?

Nurturing myself through sad days, I tuck inward and reach upward. I love being with myself, writing, musing, and climbing trees to commune with God. Hula hooping. Biking. Sitting on a rock to pen poems, escaping the cold house in more ways than one. I learn to cherish calm, value invisibility, and believe that I'll become peaceful beyond these days that feel neglectful, chaotic, and mean.

Marriage as A Container to Grow Strong

"I like steak at nine with a beer," he announces.

"I like salad with water at five," I reply.

Episcopalian and tall. Jewish and short. Fraternity. Independent. Hugely attracted to one another, which later feels karmic.

On our first wedding anniversary, I awaken with palpable excitement.

"We'll grow and change together! Isn't that great?"

"What are you talking about? I am who I am!"

My soul fizzles like air from a balloon. This is not what I imagined! Now what?

All my life, I've been sensitive, avoiding conflict, and putting others' needs before mine. I don't feel grown or strong enough to leave.

And there we are, blasting *Supertramp Breakfast in America* on the stereo, trips to the West Side Market for bratwurst sandwiches and apple fritters, reading Sunday papers on the deck, coffee for Mister, tea for me. I birth one son and then another. He manages the outside while I care for the inside. We talk over dinner and travel together until increased fear grounds me after 9/11.

Our lives move along, well-organized without chaos. After 26 years of marriage and raising wonderful sons, we relocate from northeastern Ohio to the mountains of western North Carolina.

After a year in the mountains, Mister's ruffled when I become vegan.

"I want a different life! I'm going to therapy," he declares.

"Is this about you? Is this about us?" escapes me.

His answer leaves me feeling as if nothing's solid beneath my feet.

Therapy day arrives, along with torrential rains and a salon visit gone awry. Mister's in the kitchen when I return with pizza, salad, and Goth Black hair.

"Therapy was good," he offers.

"Would you like to say more?" I ask with trepidation.

"Joy, why don't you sit down."

As he spills words that land in my gut like a black cloud, I hear a voice. *Take in this darkness. You need it. You're going to transmute it.*

Our split is painful, messy, and perfect. My sleep-addled mind spins with cognitive dissonance between who he's been and what he told me. I stay present, feeling this pain through every cell.

How can our marriage end? What about the boys? Our family unit?

Swimming in anger, I grieve the end of our union. I sink into prayerful baths, write in my journal, and give myself time to absorb this shock to my system.

I needed this journey.

I needed the separateness our marriage provided to grow into myself within a safe framework, and I needed release from a union that didn't resonate in my depths.

A Perfectly Perfect Path

When our younger son goes to Kindergarten, I have more time than I've had in years. I pray at the kitchen sink to use my writing gifts. Two days later, as I dress for a church meeting, I receive a vision; the minister will ask me to do something.

The scene unfolds exactly as I'd envisioned. Reverend Norling invites me into his office, where he asks if I'll edit the church newsletter. I'm awestruck. In time, this position lets me stretch creative muscles and more. When the secretary who types the newsletter calls me a perfectionist, I head home to write:

Perfectly

I need help. I turn to the business section of the Cleveland White Pages, scan the P-e-r-f's, and what do I find? Everything one would want beginning with Perfect Accent and The Perfect Bride all the way through precisely 48 more listings.

But the perfect listing I'm searching for doesn't seem to exist. It's perfectly clear that Perfectionists Anonymous is not to be found.

It's recently come to my attention that I'd be a perfect candidate for such a group. My attendance would be perfect. I'd always arrive on time, and I'd add perfectly cogent thoughts to the discussion when they made perfect sense. I'd be perfectly polite and put together and would volunteer to plan the perfect picnic.

"Hello, my name is Joy, and I'm a Perfectionist. I realize that I was born into the perfect family to nurture my perfectionism. My mother is a perfectionist, and my physician father is critical and demanding. They taught me to be perfectly honest, generous with others, helpful, and well-behaved.

Through her example and comments, my mom also taught me to recycle, to wonder what other people thought about me, and to look good whenever I went out. I credit my dad with teaching me to be quiet, to achieve, and to have a short fuse with my family.

In marching band, I led the flag line. I worked out perfect routines and guided my squad to perfectly march and wave their flags.

In junior high, I joined the track team, running the 440 and high jumping, winning a lot of ribbons. I quit when the pressure of perfectly competing superseded the joy of winning..."

Faith of a Different Kind

I feel uneasy about driving downtown for a newsletter interview with Faith, but I chalk it up to suburban paranoia, telling myself that I'm just nervous driving where I don't normally go. I don't interpret the feeling as a signal to cancel the appointment. With a prayer on my lips asking God to be with me, I continue.

Approaching Bridge Avenue, my brain registers that those waiting at the red light look horrified...

What I'm not privy to is that these onlookers are watching an out-of-control van bouncing off parked cars, speeding towards my vehicle.

...as a van SMASHES into the back of my Isuzu Trooper!

I remember the huge crash and then blanking out for a time. When I come to, I can tell that my car is no longer moving under my power.

Dazed. Confused. In pain. Smells of burned rubber, the sounds of scraping metal on pavement. I struggle to make sense of what's happening. I can't reach the brake, my seat's broken, and my car rolls to a stop near the curb. People run to my car.

"I was heading to work. OMG. I saw the van crash into you. I'm so sorry! I'll call for help." So many voices at once.

I'm diagnosed with a mild concussion plus neck and back soft tissue injuries.

At the police station a week later, I'm shown a burgeoning file of accidents the same day as mine, most stamped **'Fatal.'** I'm certain that being pushed through a green light as the lead car on a one-way street kept my record from being stamped **'Fatal,'** too.

My life was protected, meeting faith of a different kind.

Thriving Beyond Long-Held Beliefs

"Stay away from chiropractic as if your life depends on it!" we hear over and over.

Dad is a physician who spurns chiropractic. It is a swear word, an idea we aren't to discuss or question.

Years after my car is rear-ended and totaled, I struggle with residual pain.

"No, you guys get the Christmas tree this year. You've got this! I'll be here when you return."

When my pain rises enough, I call the doctor. He examines me, sending me to physical therapy. I'm on a pain/healing treadmill going nowhere, unable to see options. Every time I feel better, I re-tweak my back.

At our weekly *Course in Miracles* gathering, my friend Emilie says, "Look how much straighter I'm standing today. I'm thrilled! I'll give you the numbers of my chiropractor and massage therapist in case you're interested; they're great."

In case I'm interested? Wow. Emilie knows I'm plagued with neck and back issues.

And I know that while Dad convinced us chiropractic is wrong, I'm ready to find out for myself. I move ahead with trepidation into Dr. Randy Reed's office in Solon, Ohio.

"My Dad was a physician, Dr. Reed. Do you understand how hard this is for me to be here, that I almost didn't make an appointment?"

"Joy, you're taking a big step, and I get it. I assure you that I'll support your healing. You will not need to return and return. I'm not that guy," he reassures me.

I relax, trusting Dr. Reed to start treatment. By seeing him, alternating with the massage therapist Emilie mentioned, I begin to feel much better as aspects of the accident leave my frame.

From that time on, I listen more closely to my body, seeking assistance when I'm in distress, crossing bridges of other ingrained beliefs.

Like the morning I'm in a journaling class, when we're writing about how to live *Wildly*. Responding to the questions, an awareness enters that I live with white gloves on.

Edicts of my childhood echo within: *Don't do that! Be quiet! Go away!*

I'm the one holding the key to the locked chambers of my youth. I'm the one who can take off my gloves. How fun would it be to color outside the lines? I can live with more abandon.

My consciousness widens.

I twirl in front of soul sisters, proclaiming, "I'm going to take up space!"

Gems of Connection

"Where do you live, Joy?" asks a woman I've just met.

"Thanks for asking. I live in synchronicity."

A friend who knows I'm beginning to write poetry invites me to a women's writing conference at Punderson State Park, east of Cleveland, Ohio. As I drive the winding, tree-lined road to the Manor House, a thought washes over me; *I wonder who I'll see here that I know.*

Just inside the door, I encounter a woman I'd met the year before at a poetry therapy weekend. At dinner, I notice that the woman sitting next to me hails from my Israeli dancing days in Youngstown, Ohio.

The next morning as I wait for the poetry session to begin, a woman sitting catty-corner says, "You look familiar to me." I turn to see who'd spoken, exclaiming, "You're my high school English teacher!"

Unbelievable.

On every break, Mrs. Ague and I reconnect, covering the missing 27 years, finding common interests in poetry therapy, books, and family.

Two years later, Elma (she'd asked me to call her by her first name soon after we'd met) drives to my house so we can travel together to a poetry therapy weekend in Lakeside, Ohio (where, coincidentally, I'd gone to band camp in high school as a perfect flag line leader perfecting perfect routines for my squad).

Elma hadn't been able to write about her son's death to cancer seven years earlier, and she hopes to have a writing breakthrough.

Although Elma and I don't discuss her possible progress during the weekend, she seems restless and quiet as she continues to struggle with pent-up feelings aching for release to the page.

As I shower to travel home from Lakeside, the thought arrives, *you told Elma the story of your writing path, but you left out the critical piece about perfectionism she may need to hear.* On our return trip, I share with Elma how God had awakened me to confront this part of myself which led to new miracles of awareness at every turn, spiritual growth, and family healing.

She writes to me soon after, "Bill (her husband) says the weekend was worth every penny because, for the first time in 30 years, I put away the sheets without ironing them first." And Elma began writing every morning, loving her newfound voice. She also discovered a beginning place to write about the premature death of her son.

Elma and I continue to connect in various ways. When she publishes her poetry book *Scattered Pages*, Elma wows me by writing this:

Dedication
To Joy

Were you born wise
or did you find
your peace
sitting on a rock
letting the world
open you,
clarify you,
mold your soft clay
gently with
soft winds,
tree whispers,
bird songs,
silence,
till the You
of you
let loose

the shouting,

the hurting,

the piercing words

and filled your soul

instead with the peace

and love of self

and wisdom you now have?

Tell me, tell me

if you can—

for I would find my rock

and be

the Me

I know my God

has planned.

The Tool

Writing this chapter allowed me to Mine the Lessons of My Life more deeply than before, giving me new perspectives, insights, and joy.

May you experience a similar journey as you Mine the Lessons of Your Life, living into your best days!

If I can be of service, please connect.

1. Revisit Your Stories

Pull out an old journal or consider your stories. Read and reflect. Since it's years beyond your entry or memory, what hidden joys can you find? What new perspective can be revealed? That was then. This is now.

Writing this chapter led me to see that my marriage was a safe container to grow within and how much I touched Elma Ague's life.

2. Unpack What's Not Working

If your life isn't unfolding well, ask yourself what stories or beliefs run your days. We can slip into patterns, and we need to awaken beyond them.

*"What about letting go of **better** to live into best?" a friend said.*

*I mused about that, telling my **better** man that we may want to end as mates. "I've been feeling it," he said.*

*Our conscious split allowed me to live into **BEST!***

*My **BEST** partner is Michael, a man whose internal mantra was: "Life is easy for those without preferences."*

Then he happened to read a book of mine which held this poem:

Of Dreams

Rain drenches a yard,
Rivers run banks
chasing lives to higher ground,
and you do a rain dance
in your mind, gaze
upon cracked mounds of earth,
dream of water sprites.
Some dreams before yours and mine
died in silence, some spent time
behind bars, some took flight.

Awake or sleeping, we choose a path.

Wake up, my friend.
Come dream with me.

"I realized that I had buried my dreams and locked my desires behind bars. One of those desires was having a little more Joy in my life," Michael recalls.

3. Heal Separation

Separation is an illusion.

Consider your connections. Are you feeling separate from others? From God? From your soul's contentment? Is this your perception? Is it true? What healing steps can you take? Will you reach out to a friend? Bridge a void with your brother?

Loving myself, I'm more connected than ever within and without.

4. Develop and Maintain a Spiritual Practice

Spend daily time away from family, television, and all that calls. Read texts that speak to your soul. Read daybooks that raise your thoughts to higher planes. Keep a gratitude journal. Write in a journal. Breathe into silence.

My daily spiritual practice feeds my days, grounds me, and connects me with all that is. Journaling has fed my faith, healing, and writing life as an author.

5. Slow Down, Breathe, Allow

Our culture moves fast, convincing us we need to do more than one thing at a time, buy the latest and greatest, etc. Do we? Is it time for you to alter the pace of your days? Can you believe in your worth without rushing to achieve? Can you allow your partner to be more of who he/she is? Do you need to breathe in the middle of the day? Nap? Drink more water? Stretch? Wake up to honor your sweet self, dear one.

It was a path to give up adrenalin, and I'm glad I did. Not rushing rocks. So does doing one thing at a time, allowing people to speak without interrupting them, and allowing them to be who they are. Each person is a divine spark doing their best.

ABOUT THE AUTHOR
Joy Resor ~ 63

Joy Resor wrote a daily prayer for months to become the Joy she's created to be. Her life has been a ride and a half of lessons, spiritual experiences, and synchronicities. After surrendering her will to Divinity, the All (God, Source, Universe) visited, teaching this poster child of separation for over 50 years that separation is an illusion and co-creation is the way:

"...Joy, you just don't get it. With you in matter and me with the POWER of the Universe, what WE can accomplish."

Joy lives in western North Carolina where she's an inspiring author of books through her heart and hands, a contributing author in others, and an inspiring guest on podcasts and radio shows.

Ordained as an Alliance of Divine Love minister and certified in spiritual direction, she serves clients as their spiritual mentor, officiates weddings, and brings joy to everyone she meets.

Joy offers workshops to inner-city transitional youth in Pisgah Forest, NC, and participates in a prison book and letter-writing ministry. Beyond pandemics, Joy loves facilitating workshops and being a welcoming presence of love, peace, and joy at spiritual conventions as a vendor of Joy on Your Shoulders (J.O.Y.S.) Batik cotton wares and books.

Born in Brooklyn, NY, Joy lived most of her life in Ohio, where she and her husband raised two sons before moving south, followed by divorce. She loves her partner Michael, hula hooping in sunbeams, and co-creating to inspire others onward. She received her B.S. in Mass Communications from Miami of Ohio.

You'll enjoy a visit to Joy's site!

Sign up for her monthly newsletter, read articles and look around to your heart's content.

https://www.joyonyourshoulders.com

https://www.facebook.com/JoyOnYourShoulders

https://www.linkedin.com/in/joyresor/

CHAPTER 9

Seeing is Believing, Believing is Seeing

Powerful and Simple Practices for Creating Your Best Life

By Julie Ulstrup MS, Award Winning Portrait Photographer, TEDx Speaker

"Your vision will become clear when you look inside your heart. Who looks outside, dreams. Who looks inside, awakens."

—Carl Jung

My Story

¡Levantarte! GET UP bellowed the *albergue* (think AirBnB, hostel, and motel all rolled into one) owner. My sweaty back stuck to the plastic sheet on the bottom bunk as I shot to my feet. Although I was tired and hungry

after walking 15 miles across the Spanish countryside, Jose Marie had my attention. It was an unusually hot day in April hiking on the Camino de Santiago with a 30-pound pack on my back.

His voice became gentler after he admonished me for lying on the bed in my hiking clothes before showering. He was right; I needed to clean up. "After a shower, would you and your fellow travelers like a Pilgrim's Mass? I have permission from the local priest," he asked. "Por supuesto (*of course*)," I replied, knowing it would be an experience we would all accept.

I was the only Spanish speaker in the group who decided to stop at this albergue that evening and Jose Marie only spoke Spanish. We were *peregrinos*, pilgrims from the United States, England, Germany, and South Korea, walking the *Camino* path for our own reasons. Each on our own path, but on the way together.

We walked down a worn dirt path toward a small, simple, stone church that looked more like one of the pagan temples that I saw in my high school history book than the opulent cathedrals spotting the Camino de Santiago along the countryside in Northern Spain. Jose Marie unlocked the giant wooden door with an old key and led us inside.

"Nuestra Padre"

"Our Father"

"Unser Vater"

"우리 아버지" uli abeoji

Five pilgrims and Jose Marie stood at the front of the church holding hands reciting the Lord's Prayer in our native tongues before we started the Mass. We took our seats in the cool temple as the sun descended toward the horizon.

I let the words of the mass wash soothingly over me as I sat on the cold, hard church pew. Translating Spanish to English was effortless in my mind as I had been studying Spanish and become fluent in the previous five months. *My mind was appreciative.*

Although I was tired from walking between 20 and 25 kilometers each day, I was grateful. It was the good kind of tiredness, the kind you feel after you've accomplished something physically, pushed yourself a little further than you thought you could. *My body was grateful.*

The family I lived with in Spain, my *prima*, cousin (most of the students were college-aged and referred to their host as their "mom," and since we were close to the same ages, we called one another "cousin") but her family embraced me and loved me. They filled me with encouragement and a newfound sense of myself as my language skills grew every day. I dreamed of living in Europe since I was in college. This journey was thirty years in the making. *My heart was full of gratitude.*

Nearly one year earlier, I was sitting at my desk when an email came across the screen with the opportunity to apply for a sabbatical, which meant I could take up to a twelve-month leave, and my position would be held for me when I returned. Sabbatical, I would learn, is an ancient religious tradition encouraged every seven years to give the spirit a chance to explore, grow, and learn in new ways. The school district where I worked as a school counselor for the last seven years approved my request to study the Spanish language and culture to support Spanish-speaking students and their families, of which there were many in my current position.

Needing a respite from the heartbreak that was my life for the previous four years, I applied for one of the few sabbaticals offered. A brutal divorce splintered my family, leaving me feeling abandoned, shattered, and untethered. My teenage children were studying at university. This was a time for me to rediscover my soul purpose. It was time for me to step into something bigger.

Little did I realize how my life would elevate due to the experiences I had living in Spain and along the Camino de Santiago. I studied Spanish in college and even participated in a three-week immersion program in Mexico. As a first-generation American, I had traveled outside the US to visit my grandparents, as well as having the opportunity to have many other international experiences growing up and as an adult. However, I was completely unprepared for the level of transformation by the experience of living and studying in a completely different culture than that in which I was raised.

Amazing Grace how sweet the sound I heard the most beautiful song in the sweetest voice *that saved a wretch like me,* warm tears streamed down my cheeks *I once was lost but now I'm found, was blind but now I see,* tears continued to flow, tears I thought may never stop. *Twas Grace that taught my heart to fear and Grace, my fears relieved How precious did that Grace appear The hour I first believed.* They did stop, and the Mass ended.

As I left the church, my German friend waited for me at the back door. "Tobias, thank you for singing 'Amazing Grace,'" I said. "I wasn't singing and besides, that is an American hymn," he said. "But you heard it didn't you?" I knew he sang in his church choir at home. "Nobody was singing," he emphasized by crossing his arms over his broad German chest. Once again, the tears started flowing as I knew that song was divine, and for me, I needed and deserved grace. Not only did I feel divine grace in that moment, I knew I was to continue my path to elevate others to see their vision for their own life.

My Camino continued for another two weeks before I arrived at the Compostela de Santiago on Good Friday, then on Easter Sunday caught my flight back to Colorado, and my life, completely transformed by the experience. Along The Way, as the Camino de Santiago is often called, I experienced many blessings, transformative experiences, and lifelong as well as fleeting friendships that continue to shape my life.

It was a journey that my Irish friend Sioban described as *very simple and very good*. I woke each morning as the sun climbed over the horizon. Getting ready for the day, I packed my *mochilla* backpack with my clean socks, underwear, and top that I washed in the sink the night before. Each albergue owner would have breakfast waiting, and I'd be off. One foot in front of the other, across the Spanish landscape, that sometimes felt like it would go on forever and sometimes felt like it ended much too soon.

Food and laughter, drinking Spanish wine, sharing my stories, and listening to the stories of my fellow pilgrims filled my days with a holy reverence as I have never experienced before or since. On the Camino, as in life, we walk alone, yet the relationships we create, the stories we tell, the experiences we encounter, and how we respond all make our lives rich and full of expansive wonder.

Before I finished my walk on the Camino, I decided to expand my life-long passion for photography and build a portrait business to elevate others to see their strength, wisdom, power, and beauty. It's in all of us. Each. And. Every. One. Of. Us.

My entire adult life has been lived empowering others, especially women. I believe that empowered women change the world, which is why I chose to hone my photography skills and learn my craft from the very best international photographers, ultimately becoming Colorado's premier portrait photographer. I specialize in elevating women for their business branding, with their family, and in personal and social sessions.

There is a story many of us have told ourselves; I have heard one version or another of the excuses why women do not want to be in pictures. I'm certain that you know what you say in your head or even out loud when someone brings out their phone for a photo, much less if a professional portrait of you alone is suggested. Note: I'm not repeating those thoughts or words on this page to take away the power we have given them and to change the narrative we have had historically about having pictures made of ourselves. Not by ourselves, our family, or our friends.

I have heard hundreds of reasons, excuses, and declarations of playing small by women who are community leaders, authors, and matriarchs of their families. Yet I challenge you to think, have you ever looked at a photograph or a woman you love, your grandmother, mom, sister, aunt, or daughter and said or thought something negative? Of course not! Photographs of those we love become our greatest possessions and the first thing every person says they would grab if leaving their home during a fire.

There is also a false belief that some people are photogenic and others are not. This is another lie. These lies diminish our ability to be seen in a bigger way, by ourselves and by the world. If we want to live a bigger life, make a bigger impact, and share our glorious goodness with the world, we need to show up as our biggest, brightest selves.

Each of us is responsible for showing up, seeing ourselves, and being seen in the world. Nearly 90% of the information our brain processes in any moment is visual. Photographs that you love of yourself are essential to living your biggest and best life.

My decision to become a portrait photographer didn't even really seem like a decision; it seemed like a calling to elevate women in a way that I know can change their lives for the better.

The process of creating a portrait of a woman that she will love and be able to see in herself what the people who love see in her begins with a conversation about who she is and how she shows up for herself and in the world. Once we schedule a session, we talk about the details of what will make her session a phenomenal experience for her and how she wants to be seen.

Together we co-create and style a session to bring out the very best in her. My makeup artist and I style every detail before she even gets in front of the camera. From the moment we start the session until the final shot is taken, she feels and looks like the absolute best version of herself. It shows in her photographs.

When women see the images we have created, they respond with tears of joy, gasps: "Is that really me?" And exclamations: "I've never seen myself like this before!" The beauty of a portrait experience with me becomes the legacy the women create for themselves. Every time they look at the photographs, they aspire to live that very best version of themselves, looking back at them in the portrait.

The Tool

When I returned home after my Camino, a dear friend reflected upon my experiences, stating that my entire brain shifted as a result of learning a language with a different structure, cadence, and rhythm to my native tongue. While walking for 21 days on the Camino, my life became very simple and very good. With only a few belongings in my backpack, each day, I would walk, discover new places, eat and reflect on how I wanted my life to unfold every day.

Although I did not long to live my life as a pilgrim, walking and reflecting each day on how I wish to live, I do long to live a life of gratitude and a life of purpose on purpose, which is what my tool will offer. Like the Camino, it's very simple, but it's not easy.

As a child, perhaps like most of us, I was taught to be grateful, to say thank you, and when I prayed, to thank God for what I had. As my experience of learning a new language changed my brain and how I move through the world, so will this tool. This tool is life-changing as we become grateful for our vision of what we desire and what we want to manifest in our lives.

Take a 5 x 7 piece of card stock paper and fold it in half to create a tent. Write five to seven things in the present tense that you desire to become or grow in your life. For example, mine include:

I am a loving daughter, sister, mother, wife, friend, and mentor.

I am so prosperous I can afford anything I want.

Place the tent on your nightstand where you can see it every evening before you go to sleep and first thing every morning.

There are many ways this helps you to become that which you are seeking. Writing is a powerful act of declaration from your spirit to the world. It is also a powerful reminder for you when you are most aware of your deepest desires.

Each morning before anything else, write ten things for which you are grateful in a notebook. Gratitude is the gateway to your highest vision of yourself, which leads me to the biggest mindset shift of all.

After writing your gratitude list, in a seated position, begin with a square breath.

As you inhale, count to five and imagine a line going up the side of a square until your lungs are full.

Hold your breath as you imagine a line crossing the top of the square for a count of five.

As you exhale, imagine a line going down the side of the square for a count of five.

Hold your breath as you imagine a line crossing the bottom of the square for a count of five.

Repeat this square breath at least ten times. By focusing on your breath, you focus on the moment here and now. Just this moment, just this breath.

Breath is the best and easiest way to become connected with your physical body, leading to the integration of your body, mind, and spirit.

Then for the next five to ten minutes, let your mind imagine all of your deepest desires, how you want to feel, how you want to look, how you want to act, what you want in your life, who you want to be with, what you want your relationships to look like, no matter how big or how small. You are never given the desire without also being given the means to manifest the life of your dreams.

As you repeat this practice each morning, you will notice that you will also have ideas about how to make your dreams become a reality. You will notice that you are living the life of your dreams and that new dreams emerge. Write them all down so you can become the next highest vision of yourself.

This practice is simple, yet it's not easy. Mindful breath practice brings our body and mind into alignment for our highest good, which is why this is a powerful exercise any time you need a break or a boost of energy or even to relax and gather your thoughts. Often we rush through our days without intentional creation of who we want to be or how we want to show up in the world. It will become a way of life that leads you to your deepest desires, one step at a time, one breath at a time.

By creating a vision for ourselves of who we wish to become and being thankful for that which we desire, we are able to walk towards and attract that with every fiber of our being. Ancient sages, the world's wisdom traditions as well as hundreds of modern-day success stories, all attest to the power of gratitude to live the life of our dreams to fulfill our soul's purpose on earth.

ABOUT THE AUTHOR
Julie Ulstrup ~ 58

Julie Ulstrup has been passionate about photography since she was a child. As she grew, so did her love of the art and craft, encouraged by her maternal grandparents, camera store owners before she was even born. Julie lives the life of her dreams with portrait, boudoir, and business branding studios in Colorado, Southern California, and soon throughout Europe. You can experience her in her zone of genius as she styles, poses, and guides those in front of her camera through an experience of elevation and transformation. Her life's work is to elevate others especially women.

Traveling in and around the United States as well as internationally is another lifelong passion for Julie. In addition to meeting and getting to know people with different perspectives and life experiences, food and adventure make the journey interesting. Surfing, scuba, hiking, cross country skiing, riding as the stoker with her husband on their tandem bicycle, and hiking is how she spends her free time.

In addition to being a published author, business owner, and award-winning portrait photographer, Julie recently gave a TEDx talk, "Transform the Way you see Yourself," which you can view here **https://www.youtube.com/watch?v=lmlvEila1DU**

Born in the City of Angels, raised in the Windy City, Julie now calls the foothills of Colorado's Rocky Mountains home. It's here Julie lives and shares her dream of creating portraits, boudoir, and business branding photographs that bring the beauty inside out. Allowing you to see yourself in your most authentic and vulnerable light, so you can attract those who need your message to have a greater impact in the world. Julie captures not just an image but the soul.

As an empowerment photographer, Julie helps her clients to see themselves in a way they've never seen themselves before.

For more information about her work visit **https://www.julieulstrup.com**

I'd love to connect

https://www.linkedin.com/in/julie-ulstrup-7b158b18/

https://www.instagram.com/julieulstrupphoto/

https://www.facebook.com/JulieUlstrupPhotography

Julie@JulieUlstrup.com

CHAPTER 10

Warrior Journaling

Conquering Purpose-Driven Fear with a Pen

By Laura Di Franco, MPT, Publisher, 20-Time Author, Poet

"Your fear of not-good-enough is boring. What if the thing you're still a little afraid to share is exactly what someone needs to hear to change their life? Time to be brave!"

—Laura Di Franco

My Story

"Would you like to be a featured poet at Busboys in August?"

I was fifty-one when I received the invitation from my poet friend, Miss Kiane, to knock something off my bucket list—to stand on a stage at Busboys and Poets in Washington, D.C. as the featured poet of the evening and spit my soulful words into the microphone.

I read that note in Facebook messenger at least ten times. *She must think I'm good enough.* My full-body yes was paralyzed by the life-long, boring inner critic for about five seconds.

"Yes!" I typed back.

I've learned to listen and respond to the language of my soul, intuition, and body messages coming through. I've learned to conquer my purpose-driven fears by understanding the sensation of them in my body, discerning between survival fear and the purpose-driven kind, and then taking swift action when it's a yes, even when I'm terrified. I was terrified as I typed that "Yes!"

The night of August 18, 2019 was one of the best nights of my life. Not just because I stood on the stage in front of a packed house and shared my set flawlessly. But because the ride home wasn't filled with the usual self-sabotage. It was a turning point for me. It's my choice to sit in the dark alley of my conditioned mind and listen to thoughts that'll make me feel like crap or choose something better. I choose something better. And I called my mom.

"I did it, Mom!"

"Oh, that's great honey! I'm so proud of you!"

"I told you I worked with a performance coach this time, right?"

"No, I don't think you mentioned that!"

"Jeff. He's so awesome. He helped me with things like how to memorize the words, how to use my voice inflection with certain lines, and my favorite, how to let a line breathe. I really did good, Mom."

"That's so great honey. I wish I could've seen it!"

"I'll send you a couple videos later. I'll be home in about thirty minutes."

"Okay, I can't wait. Did Chris or the kids come to watch?"

"No, nobody could make it. They all had something going on."

"Oh shoot. I'm sorry, honey."

"It's okay Mom. So many of my friends came, and even some unexpected friends showed up. My poet friend, KaNikki, and her husband, Thirteen, were there. I was so excited to see everyone."

"Thirteen?"

"Yeah, like Thirteen of Nazareth. It's a stage name. They are both performance poets. I met KaNikki, and the woman who invited me to do this, Miss Kiane, at Busboys in Virginia."

"Oh, I see! Okay, honey. Let me know when you get home. And send me those videos!"

"I will. Love you, Mom."

"Love you too, Honey."

I showed up at my very first Busboys event about a year before the feature night, nauseous with performance anxiety. I arrived alone like I would many times over that year or two.

You're not good enough to stand on a stage.

What if you make a fool of yourself?

What will they think when they see you sitting alone?

What if you fuck up?

What if you can't remember your poem?

I settled down at the small, square, wooden table. "I'll have a mojito." The waiter was like twelve years old. I felt all of my fifty-one years. I'm often one of the older folks at these events. And the inner critic was playing with me, big time. The fear inside was so amped up, my palms were wet. I slid them down the front of my jeans every couple of minutes and heard, *You better go sign that list right now, Warrior!*

I pulled off my black leather coat, hung it over the chair, and made my way up from the back right corner table to the front of the stage where that bright white piece of paper stood on a music stand. *I'll go last,* I thought. I intended to listen to the other poets and get the hang of how the evening would go down.

Big mistake. By the time I counted through the fifteen poets (the number of spots there are for an evening like that), I felt my heart chiseling its way toward the ribs in the front of my chest and working on them with a rib saw. *Grey's Anatomy* anyone? I missed most of the other poets' performances thinking about my own.

I managed to move my legs when my name was called.

"Next up to the microphone, we have Laura Di Franco!" I think there was clapping.

I pulled the crumpled piece of paper out of my jeans pocket and made my way to the stage, staring at the floor. My heart had an escape plan, through my throat. I managed to swallow it back down a couple inches. I was terrified I'd have to adjust the mic. My hostess friend was just my size and thankfully that ball was right at mouth level.

"Laura Di Franco is my name and brave healing is my game!"

The crowd reacted and I smiled. I looked down at my piece of notebook paper, shaking in my right hand, and realized the spotlight shining down from the ceiling was creating a dark shadow on the page. *Fuck I can't read it!*

"How about we do some brave healing right now. I'm gonna show you how."

"Okay!" I heard one sister beyond the blinding light shout. "Uh-huh!" They were ready for this and weren't going to let me fail. I shook hard. The adrenaline had its way with my crazy-ass, terrified self. I managed to get every word out without my paper, anyway. It was the start of an addiction. The poetry people call it open mic therapy. It's the power of sharing your vulnerable self and words with strangers, doing something you're afraid of, and then surviving and maybe even getting a snap or claps, or a "woohoo" in the middle of it!

"I'm so worried I won't be able to remember the lines," I said to Jeff one afternoon. I hired him soon after I knew I'd be featuring at Busboys. I wanted to make my hostess proud. I wanted to make myself proud. We stood in my basement office delivering lines to each other, practicing adding the passion, and letting a line breathe.

"It's all about practice," he reminded me.

Over the last couple of years, I've practiced several poems to the point of memorizing them. The night in August, as the featured poet, I not only memorized the four poems I had picked out, I had the in-between performance chat and audience engagement down too. Jeff helped me lay out the whole thing and we even planned a moment when I asked someone up on stage. Since that night, I've spoken on more stages, shared my brave words, and refined my talks. I've learned from different speaking and performance coaches about what to do with the fear, how to deliver my words, and what it takes to move an audience, to help them feel something. Moving through my purpose-driven fears of not-good-enough to the point of now teaching others how to do this has been one of the greatest accomplishments of my life.

Now, when that boring voice pipes up in my head to ask me, *who are you to do this,* I have one response. *Your fear of not-good-enough is boring.* What if the thing you're still a little afraid to share is exactly the thing someone needs to hear to change their life? It's not about you anymore. It's time to be brave.

I've been writing words and poems in notebooks since I was fifteen years old. Over my career as a holistic physical therapist, I married writing and journaling with body awareness and healing and came up with warrior journaling exercises that helped me when the voice was its loudest and most paralyzing. One of my favorite Brave Healing writing exercises is an easy one, meant to help you get very clear about the messages inside, discern your survival fear from the purpose-driven kind, and get to the life and purpose you were born to live. Because with deeper awareness, we get a choice. Awareness is the key. Awareness will help you do, say, and be anything you wish to be.

If I can shift from a painfully shy young woman, afraid to speak out loud, to standing on a stage spitting poems into a microphone, you can too. The world is waiting for you to get your brave on.

The Tool

Warrior Journaling Part One

Grab a notebook and pen and draw a line down the center of the page so you have two columns. At the top of the left side column write the words, "Hell No!" And at the top of the right-side column, write the words, "Hell Yes!"

Take a moment with a few deep, pelvic-bowl breaths. Inhale deep and wide, letting your ribs expand out in all directions. Release the inhale and relax, softening your whole body into your chair. Take a few more breaths like that as you begin to ground and center yourself, settling your awareness down into your core. Feel your body. Notice any sensations. Clear your mind. Take as long as you like in this part of the exercise. Every aware moment spent noticing what you're feeling is a gift you give yourself and a direct connection to your soul voice.

Think about the moments in your life that feel like a "Hell no!" What do those feel like in your body? What sensation do you have when something is not quite right, feeling bad, or feeling like a no? In the left-hand column, begin to list all the words or phrases that come to you to describe this.

Here are a few of mine to get you started:

TIGHT

CONSTRICTING

COLD

WEAK

Now, think about the moments in your life that feel like a "Hell yes!" What do they feel like in your body? Move over to the right-hand column and make a list of all of those words or phrases.

Here are a few of mine to get you started:

LIGHT

SMILING

STRONG

WARM

When you're finished, you should have two columns of descriptive words, some for the "Hell No" and some for the "Hell yes." You're getting messages like this all day long. When you tune into the sensations and understand that language, you'll quickly be able to feel into the answers for just about everything in your life. You'll no longer need to look outside yourself to others for clarity because your inner warrior and guide will let you know what's right, good, and best for you—for every next step.

Trusting these messages is the key. Starting with the awareness so you can learn and understand the language will be how you're able to say yes or no to life. Nobody else can feel for you. You get to choose. It's time to stop saying yes when your body is telling you no. Being aligned with the language of your soul is a freedom and power you have to make sure you're living the life you were born for.

Warrior Journaling Part 2

Look at your lists of descriptive words. Now think about when you're in a situation and the answer, "I don't know" comes up. You don't feel the "Hell Yes" or the "Hell no." The thought is more of a grey area or feels like confusion.

Understand something about these moments: They aren't a "Hell yes." Moments of "I don't know," "I'm confused," and "I'm not sure," are a no, because they're not a "Hell Yes." If you look at the cheat-sheet you've created from Part 1, you'll realize that the "I don't know" moments don't have the feelings of what's on your "Hell Yes" side of the page.

"It's easier to be confused because you don't have to make a decision."

My healer at the time, a very skilled acupuncturist, was helping me understand that when I was stuck in confusion, it was my choice. I was choosing the easier route—to stay confused and not make a move. The warrior's path would be to understand the confusion is a no and take the action required for the next, best step, however difficult it seemed. I was making a huge decision about my marriage at the time. She looked at me when she said it, and there was a long pause. I had to allow the fact that I'd been taking the easy route to really sink in. This one realization has helped me feel clearer about more things in my life than ever before. Moving forward into my fifties has been one of the best times of my life because I have the most powerful tool in my toolbox— the ability to discern whether something is a "Yes" or a "No" for me, my heart, and my soul. The clarity I received listening to my intuition about what's good for me (instead of listening to the opinions of everyone else around me) was life changing. This path is not easy. But it's worth it. It takes a warrior to show up for the moments of her life and not only make a decision to go for the joy but to take the action for it, unapologetically prioritizing her health and wellness, putting that oxygen mask on first.

The thing about purpose-driven fears is that they have a lot of the "No" column feelings. That gets confusing because many of the things you truly want to do, say, and be come up as a "Hell No!" when they're really a "Hell Yes!" Let me help you take this one step further.

Warrior Journaling Part 3

To be able to discern those "Hell No!" column feelings from the purpose-driven fear feelings inside you, you can check them against the following criteria to see if they are a "Hell Yes!" in disguise.

Purpose-driven fears have qualities different from regular old "Hell No!" feelings. Here are a few questions to ask:

1. Is there always a little bit of excitement mixed in? My breathworker, Lauren, says, "Fear is just excitement without the breath!" Purpose-driven fear will always have that feeling of excitement to it, a little nudge or spark of, *oh my, I think I can do this!*

2. Does the situation present itself over and over again? Purpose-driven fears have this way of showing up over and over again because it's your soul calling to you! Time to listen! The Universe knows what you need and is in charge of the "how." Trust that what's coming up, again, is a breadcrumb to follow.

3. Is the situation something that aligns with your bigger vision and purpose? If it aligns with what you're here to do, then stop doubting and second-guessing it and take the action. Successful people do it afraid. And everyone is afraid. It's a matter of taking the action and having a little more fun with those purpose-driven fears!

These are a few of the ways to know if that feeling inside should slide to the "Hell Yes!" side of your notebook. Taking some time to journal about what that purpose-driven fear feels like inside of you will be a great start to understanding that language of your soul. The more you understand

and practice the language, the more fluent you become, and the faster you'll be headed toward the moments and experiences of the life you were born to live.

ABOUT THE AUTHOR
Laura Di Franco ~ 53 going on 18

Laura is the CEO of Brave Healer Productions, publisher of world-changing, non-fiction, holistic wellness books that support the business success of the author as much as the healing journey of the reader. She is also the author of twenty books, including *How to Have Fun with Your Fear,* a workbook to help you move through the purpose-driven fears so you can get on with changing the world. Laura is on a mission to help you share your message, story, business, and powerful tools with the world in a way that creates a thriving, healing business and legacy.

Laura is a goddess who started building her empire the day she chose joy and meant it. Realizing that unapologetically surrounding herself with the love and support she'd need to make a huge impact in the world was a turning point. She hasn't looked back since. She aims to publish 1000 wellness books before she dies and figures she'll have to make it to about ninety-four to do that.

When she's not writing, speaking poetic words, or sharing her business-building badassery, you'll find her driving her Mustang, sipping a mojito, bouncing to the beat at a rave, or walking in the woods. She's the mom of two amazing humans and two dogs. She was probably either a cowgirl or a race car driver in a past life. She healed herself by going for the joy. Ask her about that sometime.

https://www.LauraDiFranco.com

BeWarriorLove@gmail.com

Facebook: **https://www.Facebook.com/YourHighVibeBusiness**

CHAPTER 11

Posh Life or Poor House?

Living Rich When All Seems Lost

By Heidi Blair, CPCC

Dear Beloved,

What I want you to feel after reading this is the beautiful potential you possess right now at this time in your life. It's so much more potent than when you were in your twenties, thirties, and even in your forties. Your wisdom and experiences have prepared you for the best chapter of your life!

My Story

On September 29th, 2008, I had no idea what I was doing, and that that day and the cascade that followed would utterly change my life. I didn't find out about what happened until after the election. "Hi, Eileen. Clay or hardcourt today?" I asked as I signed the member's roster at our country club.

"Um, I don't have my clay shoes, so hard, okay?"

"Sure, court five is open."

"Great!"

We walked from the clubhouse under the falling snow of a typical November day in Jackson Hole, Wyoming, and through the heavy doors that kept the heat inside our winterized, literally "bubbled" tennis courts. The fans were constantly blowing to keep it aloft and allow us to play in skirts year-round.

"Heidi, how's the remodel coming?"

"The kitchen is finished, and the painting is wrapping up. I'm just waiting on the custom runner I'm having made for the staircase, and that's it. I'm thrilled it will be ready for Christmas! Did you find an apartment in New York?"

"Not yet, we're going to be there over Christmas, which is a shitty time to be looking, but so many people lost their asses in the mortgage crisis that our agent thinks we'll have plenty of choices. I'm just so glad we closed escrow on our house here before the crash!"

Crash? What? Shit! I really should watch the news. Eileen just moved out of her home in our millionaire neighborhood just one block away from me, where evidently, I was living in a bubble of my own. I had just six months until my youngest graduated high school and planned to cash in on my investment and move back to California, where you could play tennis outside pretty much year-round.

My daughter graduated in June 2009, and I turned fifty a week later. I hosted a week-long celebration in my newly renovated home for six of my high school besties in honor of us all hitting the big Five-O. They were all still working; some were talking about retirement from teaching, nursing, court reporting, and I hadn't had to work since I was twenty-eight. Divorced and empty-nesting, I was free to move on to my next chapter, which was to be a small acreage farm somewhere in the wine country.

But by then, I was semi-hiding from the truth and the reversal of fortune standing between me and the dream. *I can't believe this is happening; I'm such* *an idiot; I should have just rented for a year until Samantha graduated; why didn't I just put down 20% instead of $600,000?* I bought the house in 2007, at the height of the market, and I sunk a monster chunk of change into flipping it for a hefty profit. The boomtown of Jackson was slowly going bust as tourism slowed, jobs were lost, and businesses struggled.

Mike, my boyfriend, gave up his cush job building custom homes on Maui to come help me cash in on my cow. With that cow no longer able to give milk and all investments either lost or not worth much, we needed a Plan B.

By August, I rented out the house, we packed a U-Haul and set out for a horse farm in Bucks County, Pennsylvania, to ride out the recession. Mike's entire family was back there, and I procured for us a couple's caretaking position on a pastoral 45-acre estate with a dozen horses, a couple of dogs, and a few barn cats. It seemed ideal. We flew out to meet the couple and their young daughter, go over our employment details, and see the two thousand square-foot apartment over the gorgeous barn we'd be living in. I was enticed to bring my horse plus two dogs and a cat, as initially negotiated. The pay wasn't great at $500 a week, but the lifestyle was what lured me. I was hired as the estate manager, primarily managing the staff as well as doing some cooking. As a former B&B owner, a trained chef, and having horse knowledge, it seemed like an ideal fit. Mike would do maintenance on the many outbuildings and other projects requiring his skills.

He drove across the country in a moving van pulling my Audi station wagon, with the dogs as co-pilots. I hired a professional horse transport company to bring my mare safely to her new barn, and I flew out with the cat under the seat in front of me. We started our new life on September 2nd.

I could write an entire book about this misadventure, but let's just say, it started badly, and it ended even worse. When hired, the staff included a barn manager, a farmhand named Carl, a full-time housekeeper, and a nanny. When we arrived, only Carl was there, and the housekeeper was down to two days a week. We were gone by the end of December, and so was Mike's father. The silver lining was that Mike had time with his dad before he passed.

I gave away my beloved bay mare, Jewels, unable to afford to transport her and board her back in California. We drove west in early January and found a rental house in Marin County. As we were both unemployed during a brutal recession, I had to give the landlord four months' rent plus the deposit. I also bridged the gap between the rent I received for my house in Jackson and the mortgage, insurance, maintenance, and HOA fees. *Thank God I have tons of credit!*

Our new house was a charming Craftsman, with gorgeous built-ins and a leaded glass china cabinet that had been waiting seventy years for my dainty set of lemon adorned dishes that I bought while on a romantic vacation on the isle of Capri. I loved it! I was back in my old hometown and with my best friend Toni of over twenty-five years. I had my optimism, my determination, and my beloved Mike. I cobbled together a resume and a string of jobs. I sold summer reading programs in a phone bank from 5:00 am to 1:00 pm for minimum wage plus commission. I ran Craig's List ads as a personal chef at fifty dollars an hour, which only led to working as a server/bartender/dishwasher at posh parties in ritzy houses like those I used to attend. I didn't mind being the help, but late-night work for twenty-five dollars an hour, when I had to be up at four in the morning, was not working.

I answered an ad for a "mother's helper" for two young children. She was going through a divorce with an 11-year old daughter, and her six-year-old son had Spinal Muscular Atrophy and could not walk. I met Patricia at a cafe in Mill Valley for a first interview and met the children in their home a few days later. They were precious and polite, and I took the job. It was a split shift; 6:45 - 10:00 getting the children breakfast, packing lunches, and off to school, then back at 2:45 to get them home, make snacks, supervise homework and prepare dinner. It was kind of like being a mom without the attachment to the outcome, and within about a year, I was affectionately dubbed "Bad Nanny."

Olivia was a bright, much older than her 11 years, young lady who devoured books at a pace I had never before witnessed. Attending a Waldorf school and without any screens in the house, she would pick up a stack of books at the library on Friday, and they'd be at the bottom of the stairs on Monday. So I asked about a pile of seven while cooking breakfast, "Livie, how many of those books did you read this weekend?" "Why, all of them, of course." She spoke like Jane Austen, not a California tween. She was skeptical when I started, a bit aloof that first week, but not Cosmo; he was instantly my buddy. I would transfer him from his wheelchair to his little "Plasma Car," a low-to-the-ground scooter designed without pedals nor need for the use of legs. He would cruise around the house by pulling the handlebars side to side, and he loved it! His toys were all arranged on a low set of shelves so he could reach them himself. He had wooden swords, a felt gnome village, puzzles, legos, cards, board games, a ukulele, and books. We played Uno, built lego creations, and had sword fights, decrying things like, "Bad form Peter!" and, "I give you my word, Hook!" There was joy, purpose, and meaning in every day I spent with these children, and in time, I grew to love their mother too. We became our own kind of family, and eleven years later, we are still.

I began my coaches course that same year, in 2010. I enrolled in a year-long intensive in-person training at CTI (Coaches Training Institute) right up the road. I would attend Friday through Sunday once per month for five months and listen to audios, complete assignments in a workbook, study, practice the material with others in my cohort, and do mock sessions during the hours between my two shifts. I was learning so much, and it was a tremendous benefit to working in the role of caregiver and employee within a family dynamic with many moving parts. I went into certification with eleven paying clients, continued the rigorous course of study, the written and oral exams, and was certified in January of 2011!

My fifties were off to a fabulous start, and I imagined I would grow my practice and eventually leave the family. But that was not what the Universe divined. I coached between shifts and in the evenings. Patricia, who was on the school board and several other committees, took on an enormous project, building a fully accessible house and guest house with all the latest technical design and equipment so that Cosmo could be in a home where he could grow up and thrive. It became so time-consuming that I would become a full-time household manager and given an excellent salary to take care of all the details of a single mother's hectic life. The choice was not difficult. Honestly, it was a calling. Cosmo began spending every Wednesday night with Mike and me, then every other weekend, and sometimes more. We indulged him in action movies, cartoons, and late nights. This rule-bending wouldn't have gone over well with his mom. Eventually, we worked that out and hence the moniker, "Bad Nanny." Mike never had children, and so we had a part-time family too. My children began to refer to Cosmo and Olivia as my "other children," and Patricia used to say jokingly, "Poor dears, they have two mothers!" And honestly, even though Olivia has graduated from college and Cosmo will be eighteen next month, I will always have five children in my heart.

By 2014 the houses were complete, and I moved into the cottage alone. I had never lived alone, and although it was crushing for Mike, I made the difficult decision to experience this autonomy at fifty-four. We spent weekends together, and it was truly romantic. He would bring me roses from his garden wrapped in newspaper, accompanied by fresh fruit and veggies, and we would cook and dance in the kitchen, often singing to each other off-key. The following year, we married during a magical adventure to Europe and a slow cruise down the Dalmatian Coast to wedding day bliss at a winery on Mount Etna's slopes in Sicily. At fifty-six, wearing white lace and layers of tulle, I was a joyful bride exchanging vows with my forever love.

That same year, Patricia and I created and opened a boutique in downtown Mill Valley. Originally the concept was a co-working space for women, and we branded it as "Office Hours," but the town had pat rules about the space we leased, and we were restricted to "vibrant retail." Switching gears to combine my love of vintage furniture and Patricia's elevated sense of style, we created a museum-Esque shop filled with everything stunning, from pencils to briefcases to an all-steel and brass roll-top desk from the turn of the 20th century. Our elevator pitch was, "Everything that goes to or lives in the well-appointed office." It was the talk of the town, and a famous interior designer wandered in one day exclaiming, "What is this place?!" in a heavy British accent. She later interviewed me for a design magazine article, and we were on our way! We lasted two years and five months. Retail was dying, and literally, it rested on Jesus to keep us afloat with Christmas sales. In 2017 Patricia's mother passed, and with Olivia at Edinburgh University, she and Cosmo moved back east to be with the rest of their big family. She rented out her property, and after almost two years of marriage, I moved back in with Mike. I closed the shop in April of 2018 and cried when I turned in the keys.

I became an accidental antique dealer, moving unsold merchandise from the store through a fabulous collective emporium in Sonoma. I carried on in various posts; personal assistant, interior designer, project manager for remodels, private chef, and coaching. Weaving my multi-layered skillset into an income stream until, at sixty, I landed what I thought was my "dream job." A prominent couple hired me as their property manager to oversee their three residences and manage their newly acquired mansion's extensive remodel just ten minutes from my home (in the same town I fled to prevent my children from growing up entitled).

I was working with architects, contractors, and the principals on every phase of this fantastic project. I knew the estate; I had attended a party there, and this job was solid gold! Six-figure, full benefits, swank offices, truly work that felt like a buffet in a fine restaurant, and at the end of a long day, I kept working. Sourcing vintage and antique pieces, reviewing design elements, and excited to share with the team the treasures brought back from the hunt! Hello Covid-19. Goodbye to any buffet. As the red map bled across Asia through Europe and into California from both coasts, an unstoppable freight train wrecked it all as shutdowns, closures, and heavy restrictions sent my boss into a tailspin. A familiar face and a stranger met me on a Zoom call in June, and I knew what was coming, unemployment.

Mike and I were on the cusp of buying the aforementioned small acreage farm, and the dream. I sold my house in 2012 for a $750,000 loss. In 2013 I filed Chapter 13 bankruptcy. In 2016 I paid off the obligations. In 2020 I regained good credit, the black mark gone from my record. I'm not going to lie; the job loss was a massive blow. I spent a month in depression, escaping to "Heartland" with daily binge-watching fourteen seasons and pretending to be a teenage horse whisperer in majestic Alberta, Canada. Mike would check in on me with sweet texts throughout the day. "Are you in Canada, darling?" "What would you like for dinner?" "I bought more tissues; they're on the stairs." When I wasn't in Canada, I was in my head. *Now what? A practical person would not have gone on an extravagant holiday with no retirement. I should never have listened to Lorraine (my CPA); I knew the housing market would recover.* It did, within two years. *You should have held on; you'd have over a million in equity. Fuck! I'll never get another job like that!* That was my fear-based inner critic gnawing away at my life choices. I thanked her for her input and told her to take a cheap Greyhound bus right out of my unconventional but serendipitous and never dull life.

I got busy reinventing my coaching practice. I wrote my first published chapter in another collaborative book for women, "Find Your Voice ~ Save Your Life." I have co-created another business concept with a brilliant millennial who has become a beloved friend. And I gained clarity through the struggles of navigating through all of this during the pandemic. The epiphany! *Heidi, you already have a farm. It's in your backyard. Grow where you are planted.* All of my life experiences, risk-taking, triumphs, and epic fails, have made me a richer person and coach. Who better to guide women who believe this chapter in their life is the end of the line? Far from it!

Dear Wonderful Woman, whether you have a fat retirement or are starting over, in an unhealthy relationship with a partner or *yourself*, thinking there is nothing left to do, I assure you, there is. I implore you to examine your passions, revisit your dreams, and I am confident that you have every reason to grab these years with both hands and mold them into the life of your soul's desire.

The Tool

Tally up all of your riches (not just money), family, friends, the beautiful memories you have amassed in your lifetime. Write them down. Read them every day. And add new ones.

Make an insane bucket list, and do one as soon as possible, and then another, and don't stop.

Passion into purpose. Do what you love and make it a business, or give it away.

Dear Beloved,

Where there is fear, choose bravery. When there is doubt, chose trust. When you're in lack, look for abundance. When you're lonely, call a friend. Nothing is lost; the whole world is out there waiting for you to find yourself living in it.

ABOUT THE AUTHOR
Heidi Blair ~ 62

Heidi Blair, CPCC, lives just north of San Francisco. She is passionate about life and guiding women to really *live* theirs. To inspire them to take chances, make big changes, embody their full potential, and that age is gift! Are you at a point in your life where you just don't know what's wrong, or you do know, but you don't know what to do about it? Is that little voice inside of you trying to be heard? Is she whispering sweet wisdom, and the big voice in your brain is telling her to shut the hell up? I know. I've been there. And I wrote a chapter about it in the book "Find Your Voice ~ Save Your Life" Ultimately, I made radical life changes by listening to our quintessential gift of intuition. Integrating intuitive knowing with cognitive reasoning will captain your ship while navigating the ever-changing sea of life. If you're a woman on auto-pilot, feeling lost, stuck, or at a crossroads, and you're ready to step into the life you've imagined, I am here to help you hoist your sails and watch you cruise into a whole new world. My role is to awaken women to their innate wisdom. To ignite a spark and inspire her to examine a wider set of choices than she ever imagined. Fully embracing the magic of the next chapter in her life, like a book she just can't put down. Find Heidi at:

https://www.heidiblaircoaching.com

https://www.facebook.com/heidi.blair.59/

https://www.facebook.com/heidiblaircoaching

CHAPTER 12

The Courage To JUMP

Dare to Dream, Commit to Your Life, and Take Inspired Action

By Dr. Zora, Speaker, Thought Leader, Holistic Life Catalyst

"When you come to the edge of all the Light you know and are about to step off into the darkness of the unknown, faith is knowing one of two things will happen. There will be something solid to stand on, or you will be taught to fly."

—Anonymous

My Story

Driving on a long, open highway with the convertible top down, I was halfway through a four-hour drive in the flat plains of Colorado. The sun was shining, and there was not another car in sight.

Seemingly in the middle of nowhere, I noticed a sign for a wooded park up ahead. Great time for a stretch break! The small Park Center building was surrounded by old wooden picnic tables with a few folks relaxing and chatting.

I chose the center, well-worn path and began to walk, surrounded by large trees and scruffy sage brushes. Nature was just what I needed! This trip was not just a vacation; it was a time for deep soul searching and big decisions.

I heard the faint sound of rushing water. It wasn't long before I noted a small, barely perceptible path that disappeared into the trees to my left. That path beckoned to me with the increasingly loud sound of a quickly moving river. I love water; being around it, in it, swimming, scuba diving, on a boat, you name it!

Little did I know this place had a lesson in store for me.

I couldn't help but notice a large, black bird squawking and diving towards the ground, then swooping back up. *What's all the noise about?* I wondered. I headed toward a large tree that had fallen with the trunk stretching out at least 20 feet over the rushing water. Suddenly the bird swooped down again, and I see it lifting a little squirrel slightly off the ground but then dropping it. The squirrel scurried as fast as it could, darting one way, then another.

My heart started beating fast; my body began to shake. *Run squirrel, run!* The determined bird was relentless, no matter which way the squirrel ran. Jumping onto the horizontal tree trunk, the squirrel scurried out toward the water, then doubled back as the feathered hunter dove yet again and again. As the bird circled above, the squirrel hurried once more out onto the tree trunk, getting close to the end where the water was rushing loudly underneath.

One more swoop. With nowhere else to go, the squirrel leaped into the flow! It was gone in a split second.

Oh no. Whisked away so fast, it could never have survived. No matter what direction it tried to run, no matter how it twisted and turned, no matter what it did, nothing worked until it jumped. The drama was disturbing. Why was this affecting me so deeply?

I walked quickly back to my car, not noticing the people at the picnic tables. I simply couldn't shake the feelings. I was glad I still had a couple of hours to drive: time to feel, time to think.

I had come to visit with friends in Colorado for a three-month "sabbatical." My mentor, Tom, suggested it; in fact, he insisted. Life was challenging in many ways, and he was helping me navigate some difficult situations. I was fried, and he knew it. I knew it.

Even with the gnarly pit in my stomach from the scene I just witnessed, I loved the feeling of freedom as I drove, wind in my hair, the sun still shining. Then it dawned on me. That was it! I felt like that squirrel! No matter what I did or tried, I couldn't fix things; I couldn't change things. Life felt like that big, black bird. Then again, to be honest, I was the bird too, my inner critic, my fears pecking away at me.

I had a call scheduled with Tom the next day and couldn't wait to share this story. I described the scene at the park with all the particulars of the drama as I felt it: the relentless bird, the squirrel trying to save its own life. "And then," I shared with passion, "THE SQUIRREL JUMPED IN!"

I paused.

"Susan, don't you know?" Tom queried. "Squirrels are good swimmers! It will be fine."

"What? Really?!" I imagine my face cocked sideways with a puzzled look, like a dog on the front of a greeting card.

"I'm a good swimmer!" My body relaxed, and something deep in me shifted.

Three weeks after I got back home to Pennsylvania, I jumped. I left my marriage. I swam. I didn't die.

You are all better swimmers than you know. If you don't swim, you might fly! You can learn to trust, and be carried and supported, as the river did for the squirrel. I offer this simple tool to help!

The Tool

We are being asked to let go of all we have known. The belief that we have control is glaringly false. It never really was the case, just an illusion we're invested in. Leaving erroneous ideas behind, we open to the guidance that has been there all along. It is in us, around us, and ripe for our attention.

There is a moment where your brain has no idea what's next, no previous experience from which to discern safety or lack thereof. It's a leap, unlike any other you have had to find the courage to face before. "How can I know whether this is the right time to jump or if I'm making a big mistake?" You ask.

As we attune to the divine intelligence of the body, we attune to the whole. Let's take a journey IN.

1. Let Your Legs Carry You.

Imagine yourself standing at the beach on a sunny day. Remember the feeling of scooching your feet into the sand and the comfort of the warmth and weight? It's akin to imagining yourself as a willow tree, deeply rooted and able to flow with the wind. Or seaweed rooted in the seabed dancing with the waves. Notice the stability of your legs and the earth supporting you.

2. Allow the Breath.

Rather than sucking air through your mouth or nose down into your lungs, breathe from the bottom up. But that's anatomically impossible, isn't it? Bear with me and give it a try!

With your attention on your feet, allow an inhalation that comes up through your legs, in through the pelvis, and fills your lungs from the bottom up. Hold that breath for a few seconds, then allow a relaxed exhalation out and back down to the earth. At the end of the exhalation, stop. Wait. You have nothing to do. Your body will breathe you. Another inhalation will just come. Repeat.

3. The Brain in the Belly Informs You.

The "brain in the belly" has an intelligence of its own. Energetically we often call this gut feelings and intuition. Deep in the pelvis is an energy center where wholeness flows through you. Place your attention in the pelvic bowl and rest there. It may feel like coming "home." What do you notice? Are there messages there for you?

4. The Heart Guides You.

With your next breath, place your awareness in your heart. It's beating with ease, and you don't even have to think about it! Even if you are in a lousy mood, feel something you appreciate, care about, and love. Hold on to that feeling. Your heart's energy expands out in all directions. What guidance does your heart have for you?

5. The Mind Nurtures You.

Finally, we rise up to the mind. This crazy place where often worry and overthinking runs rampant! Left alone, it can get you into trouble, yet when deeply aligned and connected with the rest of the body, it will integrate.

Thoughts of not being good enough or old beliefs and perceptions that no longer serve you can't be sustained when run through the whole system.

THE ANSWER TO "HOW DO I KNOW WHEN TO JUMP?!"

Remember, your body thinks and feels. It's both a resonator and the suit in which you walk through your life. One of the reasons we are in such dire straits on this planet is that we have a top-down society. We honor the head and have essentially disconnected to what goes on below the neck. When decisions are made only from the head, devoid of the participation of the heart and guts, that's a lot of missing information!

As I learned to walk through life in a more present and embodied state, things looked different. In fact, I actually physically started walking differently! In years past, people would say, "oh, you walk like your father!" That wasn't a compliment. That meant I was leading with my head, shoulders a bit forward, with a determined stride. It wasn't very feminine or relaxed, but I never noticed.

I practiced embodiment techniques, cleared some old beliefs and traumas, and took responsibility for everything in my life. I started to stand up straighter, looking ahead instead of towards the ground. I began to initiate movement from my pelvis, letting my legs carry me forward rather than my shoulders.

I began to speak not from my face but more from the depths of my being. I learned to speak my truth with love.

Instead of "figuring things out" in my head, I trusted my body and integrated its messages.

Let's put it all together:

Feel your feet in the warm sand, your legs stable and strong, grounded and connected with the earth.

Breathe from the bottom up, filling the lungs with ease. Hold a few seconds.

Allow the long exhalation down through the legs.

Allow the body to initiate the inhalation.

Place your awareness in the pelvic bowl, the brain in the belly. Breathe.

Connect up and move your attention to your heart; feel gratitude for even the smallest things.

Continue up to include the head, the mind, the thoughts, and whatever else is flying around there!

From this alignment, feel the whole of your being from the ground up. Take a few steps forward, allowing your legs and pelvis to lead. Think about the over-emphasis of this on the fashion runway! What would change if you moved through your day like this?

As you practice, it only takes a moment to check in and reconnect in your body.

It's from this state of awareness that you will find the courage to jump. When you feel supported by life, trust the flow, honor your intuition, and engage the heart, a deeper knowing will be available to you.

There are little leaps and big jumps. Does it make life easier? Usually yes, other times maybe not. But one thing for sure is that YOU are present and being the best you in the world.

When you jump, the river will carry you. You may be swept quickly down the stream; other times, you will be deposited gently on the side to rest and jump back in when you are ready. If you need support, you may find that you feel a fallen branch beneath the water, which gives you a place to stand for a moment before moving on.

Surrender can feel like a scary word. Trust isn't easy, "bad" things can happen. Yet, you get to decide how you will respond. When we are truly IN life, letting go of control allows amazing things to happen. Possibilities that you never anticipated appear. Around the next turn is something beautiful. You are more open to life's lessons and the richness of the experience.

Dare to dream bigger, commit to your life, and take inspired action.

Thank you, beautiful souls, for being here on this planet now. We are in for quite a ride together!

I Don't Know...

What if you stopped for a moment?

Really, stopped.

Turned off the news.

Shut down the computer.

Put down the To Do list.

Got quiet.

Took a deep breath and a long exhale...

What if, for just a short while, you allowed yourself to not have to change anything.

For just a moment you don't have to fight for a cause.

You don't have to decide what's wrong or right.

What if for a moment, you simply said,

"I don't know."

The sun is shining, there is a gentle breeze that flows right through you.

Trees offer their strength and beauty - you can feel them.

There is more quiet outside than noise.

Inside you, there too is quiet,

If you stop long enough to feel it.

It is there that you will find yourself again.

A silent still place of peace

Where all is known, and you don't have to know.

(Dr. Zora 6/8/20)

ABOUT THE AUTHOR
Dr. Zora ~ ageless 65

 A healer in every sense of the word, Dr. Zora serves as an instrument of positive change, compassion, and well-being worldwide. A sought-after speaker, author, and holistic life catalyst, she brings her extensive experience and training together as she guides people of all ages toward self-love and self-care; connecting with earth and spirit; and living consciously and authentically.

For over 30 years, Dr. Zora owned a thriving multi-practitioner holistic health center that provided a nurturing, caring atmosphere for wellness and healing. As a Chiropractor, her loyal clientele would enthusiastically recommend her as "knowledgeable," "kind," "intuitive," and "exceptional."

Currently, Dr. Zora focuses on writing, speaking, facilitating workshops, and helps people achieve physical and emotional breakthroughs as a certified NET Neuro-Emotional Technique practitioner—a system that releases stress held in the body/mind. She intuitively helps clients hold their presence even in discomfort and inspires people to transform limiting beliefs and embrace their true passion and purpose.

Never one to shy away from sharing her own experiences and vulnerabilities, Dr. Zora brings a refreshing candor and sense of humor to life.

She is a facilitator of The Embodied Present Process, Neuro-Emotional Technique, Mind-body Medicine/Holistic Health, The Art of Feminine Presence, Laughter Yoga, and more. In addition to her Doctor of Chiropractic degree, she has a BS in Human Biology and BS in Rehabilitation Education and Counseling.

Now is the time on this planet for the human spirit to rise. Dr. Zora's mission is to help bridge the deep separations we have created, to help us transmute fear. We owe it to humanity to heal, stand in our sovereignty, our power, and true essence. Every one of us is needed, and every one of us matters.

DrZora.com, call/text 215-736-3803, or **rockstar@DrZora.com**.

Mention this book when you connect to schedule a 30 minute no-charge discovery session with me personally. I'd love to support you in a life you love.

CHAPTER 13

Lead from Within

Unleash your Intuitive Superpower for Confident, Courageous Success

By Françoise Everett, MS, Feminine Leadership and Lifestyle Coach

"The most courageous act is still to think for yourself. Aloud."

—Coco Chanel

My Story

"There has to be more to life than this!" I exclaim out loud in my office at work. I spring up suddenly from my chair. A flash of realization jolts me as I stand there looking straight ahead, and I see my life, day after day, week after week, year after year, with no difference in sight.

When I turn my head slightly and look back over my left shoulder, I see the origins of everything I can see looking forward. It's an infinite continuum of sameness.

And it scares me to death. If ever I have had a panic attack, this is it!

I was 12 years in at a top global management consulting firm, and I loved it. I loved the people, the organization, the intelligence of those around me, the prestige too. As a matter of fact, starting work there at age 25, I sort of grew up there. And the benefits: four weeks of vacation, healthy bonuses, profit-sharing, best health insurance ever, flexibility, first-class travel. In my mind, I had a pretty dreamy situation. I was well-regarded and well-respected. And I had no idea that my entire identity was tied into my perception of myself as part of a prestigious organization.

Working there was ideal. Perfect in so many ways. My pretty life packaged neatly with a beautiful bow on it.

Yet in that moment, suddenly, all that mattered so much and all that I was so proud of lost its importance.

"I want to quit my job!" I declare to my husband that evening. At this point, I believe *he* has a real panic attack. "What? Why would you want to do that?" he says in disbelief.

Yet my soul is jumping up and down. Do it, do it. Not out of desperation, but rather out of exhilaration of stepping into the unknown with a sense of confidence, curiosity, and trust. Which is interesting because even though I was a yoga student for five years, I'm not sure that I had become all that aware of my soul's desires, yet. I was never one for rash or impromptu decisions, yet here I was making one. Little did I know this was the beginning of a whole new context for my life. But it was.

So now, fast-forward ten years.

I'm at a total heart-wrenching breakdown point. I've been on an entrepreneurial journey for a few years. A lot has changed. I'm now divorced. And that identity that was so tied in with my corporate self is still seeking to find itself in this new context.

So here is the moment that leads to a real shift of finally leading myself from within, gently, effortlessly, and powerfully.

It's the middle of the night. I remember it like it was yesterday. It's late May. I'm on the top floor of my beautiful apartment overlooking the town square.

I'm in a desperate moment. I'm in bed, and I'm very thirsty.

I'm using the last of my physical energy in an attempt to reach a glass of water on my bedside table. The mind-over-matter voice in my head says *try harder*, but it's not working. My efforts lead me nowhere.

All I have to do is just roll over and reach for it. Simple right? Yet I can't. I can't move at all. I've been working to exhaustion. Overwhelm. Work hard, collapse. That's the cycle I'm in. And I've burned out to where I can't even reach the glass of water.

The water is all I want and I can't even reach *that*. I'm physically depleted.

In that moment of not being able even to pick up the water, I suddenly realize it's also impossible for me to succeed as an entrepreneur through these repeated cycles of effort, struggle, and exhaustion, no matter how hard I try.

"You must take action like your life depends on it," experts tell us. "Because if you don't, you're lazy, and you lack motivation; you don't really want it badly enough." Yet this time, this particular night, I'm so exhausted I can't even pull myself up to get the glass of water on my bedside table. And beyond desperately needing water, I no longer even *feel my desires*.

I have given it my all, and I don't have much to show for it.

Nothing is as it should be. My thoughts overwhelm me.

So I just stop trying. I surrender. In that moment, I begin to feel release from what I've named *performance paralysis;* habitual hesitation, indecision disorder, no-boundary burnout. This was from a woman who used to feel clear, confident, and courageous with a sense of adventure. In that moment of surrender, the paralysis dissolves. In that small window of release, without knowing how, I decide to recover myself. Time slows, and then I fall asleep.

The next morning, I wake up with an amazing clarity that leads me to be still until I can take each step with *mindfulness, quality,* and *excellence,* rather than massive action. I make my way to the French doors in my bedroom and look out over the town square, now washed in the morning light. I open the doors and let the sun shine on me. I see the rays traveling from the sun towards me and then back to the sun, like an infinite dance in the field of the cosmos, and I smile. I feel the warmth of the sun on my face. I close my eyes as the sun touches me and bathes me in glorious morning light. I feel held. In the moment, I realize I'm made of the same substance as the sun and the rays. We are manifesting in different forms, but we are the same, of the same Source.

Up until this moment, for most of my life, I had listened to others. I had taken on their points of view, their teachings, their templates, believing that all of them if I tried them and worked hard enough, would serve to grow my business. I worked hard, but those templates, teachings, and beliefs did not work for me. They were not aligned with who *I am*. In the process of trying all these different methods, I lost myself. I lost confidence. I depleted not only my self-trust but my own identity.

Traditionally, leadership has to do with causing another to follow, but what about *leading yourself*? How often do you cause *you* to go *your* way, and how often do you cause yourself to go *against* yourself? Think about the choices you make every single day, moment by moment.

Even with the best of intentions, you can lead yourself out of alignment with your power and natural essence.

It's easy to lose that which guides you to your most inspired, most energized Self. It's easy to fall into a cycle of taking more action, working harder, struggling just to get over the next hurdle.

Think of it this way. Everyone is showing you what you need to do: how to become a more profitable entrepreneur, how to take more action, do more stuff, fill up your calendar, increase your productivity, how to stay motivated, and how to implement strategies to advance your business or career, *and* how to have the right mindset while you're doing all that.

It is easy to find a leader with formulas, templates, strategies, and practices. But no matter how shiny those objects, for me, there was still this one missing piece—what I have come to know as *personal leadership*. None of those other components taught me how to become a better leader of my own Self, of my own life, and my wellbeing. And most importantly, of my own *neglected desires*.

Most of us have enough determination to make things happen some of the time, but eventually, if what you do every day is not in alignment with you, you'll notice that you'll begin to experience performance paralysis because you're going against who you are, your true essence and your purpose. And most of all, you'll lose your self-trust, your ability to navigate towards your own north star. This can lead you to start looking around for techniques and systems to change your results, to change you. But there's nothing to fix about you. There's only the uncovering of your natural personal leadership style. You have it already inside of you.

Yet almost all we are taught is about *doing*—that to succeed, you must do this and do that, or *not* do that. And we go all out to take on the *doing*. Massive action.

That's kind of what happened to me. I lost sight of who I am.

And eventually, I ended up in performance paralysis, not even able to reach over for a glass of water.

Waking up that morning, I slowly begin to *be*. To come from the wholeness of who I am, from the same substance as the sun. After all, there was nothing left to *do*. "To know thyself is the beginning of wisdom," Socrates famously said. And that—*your wisdom*—is precisely what is available to you when you do know yourself.

The next morning as I wake up with a new sense of clarity, I see that many other women are bumping into these same frustrations and soul-draining realities without a readily available practical means of transforming. It has now become my mission and my passion to serve the needs of just those women.

There's a way for you to become a woman who lives in flow, who knows the right next step for herself, who is confident, who understands when things are in alignment with who she is and when they're not, who knows how to make decisions and how to navigate life to create even more success. You can do this without feeling you have to push, drive, and deplete yourself to exhaustion.

So, what I'm about to share with you will change how you approach your life and your career—and, most importantly, how you approach yourself. I discovered that success does not need to lead to exhaustion. It does not have to be about forcing things uphill, feeling out of balance and out of alignment with myself in my life. I found that success is not about being busy and feeling like you're spinning a half dozen plates and putting out fires at every turn; all that leads to exhaustion.

A better way is through personal leadership, not in the masculine way, which mostly tells us to take action. Rather a leadership that brings in the feminine part of you. That part has been subjugated in the workplace. Work is traditionally based on the masculine approach of direct action. Nothing wrong with that. But when you work from the feminine part of you, allowing you to be yourself, you more often—and more easily—tap into your intuition and wisdom. You become able to receive those insights meant *just for you*, the feminine part of you which elevates everything you do, helps you to take action in a more elegant way that feels more totally aligned and graceful. You begin to see yourself with compassion, without judgment.

Slowly you begin to reinvent success. You create success *your* way without having to be something or someone you're not.

I will share a meditation to help you experience yourself as connected to and part of the larger field of life, of infinite intelligence, so you increase your capacity to act in faith and develop clarity, confidence, and trust.

Finally, I invite you to redefine success beyond the masculine paradigm of merely achieving power and money to a definition that comes from the wholeness of who you are. I want to introduce you to a success that supports from within: effortlessly realizing your deepest desires, experiencing the expansion of happiness, and the achievement of worthy goals, *all in alignment* with who you truly are.

The Tool

I invite you to discover for yourself what you are truly made of. We're going to do this through a guided meditation where you'll connect through your senses, journal with powerful questions, and then energetically activate your path to fulfill your desires.

Part 1: Meditation

Imagine feeling the sun on your face. The warmth, the beauty. The energy, the life force. Feeling the sun on your face, let it wash over you, bathe you. You can imagine yourself lying at the beach, or lounging at the pool, or as I did that morning, standing by the open French doors, receiving the sun's rays as they reached out to touch me. Feel the touch of the rays. Feel the connection between you and the sun. See the rays traveling between you and the sun. Feel the infinity of the sun's existence.

Feel the energy restoring your vitality, infusing your cells with a refreshed vibration, beginning to recognize the truth of who you are. You are made of the same substance that is beaming on you. Sense the profound truth of who you are. The one who has wisdom, a deeper knowing, love, appreciation, connection to something richer, to something greater. Infinite potential, infinite possibilities.

As you feel the immense, infinite power, take a deep breath in and slowly exhale. Take another deep breath in, all the way down into your belly, and slowly breathe out. Again, with the essence of the sun, take a deep breath in, all the way down into your belly, into your hips, down to the soles of your feet, and into the earth. Feel the connection between you and the earth, between you and the sun, and from this place of wholeness and awareness, slowly shift to your journal.

Part 2: Journaling with Expanded Awareness

In order to fulfill your dreams, desires, and achievements, you must participate in life in a new way. So often, we set our intentions and goals from sitting on the surface, and then we strategize on how to achieve them. But this often won't work.

Intention, sincerity, and expanded awareness will help you close the gap between where you are and where you want to be, more accurately, who you want to become. Be present. Open yourself to receive the wisdom meant just for you, and you will begin to cultivate your intuitive superpower. Be open, receptive, and curious about what you most desire. Listen for the answer.

What do I most desire to achieve that has personal meaning for me?

What do I most desire to experience in my life, health, career?

What do I most desire to create with deep sincerity?

What do I most desire to connect with, leading myself from within?

What do I most desire to feel alive about in my life right now?

What do I most desire to unleash and let out, which would bring joy?

What do I most desire from cultivating my intuitive superpower?

Who do I most desire to become as my fulfilled, future Highest Self?

Part 3: Embodiment

Now, I want to invite you to connect your soul, mind, and body together. Sit comfortably in a chair or on the floor with your legs crossed. Place your hands on your thighs or your knees with the palms of your hands facing up. Take a deep breath in for a count of three. Hold for a count of three. Then slowly breathe out to the count of three. Do this sequence again two more times. Having your attention on your breath helps you connect your internal and external existence.

In this expanded awareness, allow yourself to go even deeper into your body. Stretch your arms to the side. Feel the stretch from your shoulder blades all the way down your arms, wrists, hands, and fingertips. Slowly begin to raise your arms towards the sky. Notice the energy flowing through your torso as you feel the active engagement of the stretch. You have activated your meridian channels for the flow of Chi energy in your body.

When you're ready, bring your arms back down and place your hands on your thighs if you are sitting in a chair or back down on your knees if you are sitting on the floor with your legs crossed. Take a deep breath in, and slowly breathe out three times.

Slowly bring your palms towards each other in front of your chest. Close your eyes, and rub your palms together to activate energy between them. Slowly separate them and feel the energy flowing between your palms. This might feel like a tingling sensation or a pulsing sensation, or like the thickness of honey as you pull your hands apart and move them back closer together without touching. There is no right or wrong way to do this. There is just to notice and to play with this energy for as long as you feel like it.

When you feel ready, recall one of the desires you identified from journaling. Bring this desire into your energy ball between the palms of your hands, and allow your desire to merge with the energy. Slowly raise your energy ball above your head, and bring your energy ball at the top of your head down through your crown chakra, all the way through and around your body. Notice your desired experience become embodied. Bring your hands back down to rest on your thighs. Slowly open your eyes. Take a deep breath in, and slowly breathe out.

You are a woman with a beautiful, precious life, ready to become the leader of your own desires.

For a free, expanded experience of these tools, visit **francoiseeverett. com/resources**.

ABOUT THE AUTHOR
Françoise Everett ~ 53

Françoise Everett helps women around the world unlock their inner wisdom, feminine power, and hidden richness to foster success in all areas of life, from work to wealth to their own wellbeing. Her clients call her a 'catalyst for calm.'

Her work spans over 15 years in professional services and 12 in success coaching. She holds an MS in Communications Management and is a Divine Living Certified Coach. She works with both women entrepreneurs and those that hold leadership positions in large corporations across the U.S., Europe, and Australia.

Women are individuals, each with unique goals and circumstances. Her transformative coaching approach (as distinct from traditional, goal oriented coaching) helps women break through their own inner glass ceiling to define their leadership style and identity. That identity is what informs our expectations, behaviors, choices, and decisions across all parts of life. Through her transformative coaching process, women align their whole lives with their true selves.

She works in partnership with her clients to examine the areas of life that really matter: confidence, prosperity, creativity, and health, to name a few. Unlocking the key to just one of these can lead to great success in all of the others. More importantly, it can eventually lead to self-actualization, one of the most important elements of a fulfilling life.

She is the mother of an amazing daughter, lovingly adopted from China, who was the catalyst for her own growth. When not spending time with her daughter or fiancé, you can easily find Françoise in the kitchen creating her favorite paleo desserts.

After all, life is more than squeezing out that last drop of sweat and one more push-up. It's about discovering that you have the keys to a luxury life in your purse that were there all along.

You can connect with Françoise at http://francoiseeverett.com

CHAPTER 14

Inspired Wealth

Creating an Intentional Plan for Your Money

By Meredith Sims, Financial Advisor

"Money is a tool. Prosperity is a state of consciousness."

—Vanda Teixeira

My Story

For a long time, I had a vision of what my life would look like, though not the details. This was literally a vision of myself standing in a beautiful sunlit space, with a child in hand, looking out at the ocean. The light was clear, bright, yet soft and serene. The closest I came to this beautiful place was when I was visiting a home near Miami. Wealthy but simple, white walls given over to displays of art and an incredible feeling of peace gazing from the back patio over the bay. If you think of vistas in the Greek Islands, you can sense what this was like.

This vision was not a match for my life. Despite being a lover of the ocean, I had been landlocked in Atlanta, Georgia, for over 20 years. And although I once thought I would take the normal trajectory of getting married and having kids, time and circumstance meant I was single with no children.

I was dreading 50, and then, suddenly, it was my 50th year, and those fears went away. I cannot tell you why; I just felt different; I also felt relieved of any pressure to 'look' younger. I was 50! No point arguing about it or pretending anything less. What a relief! My 50th year was one of celebration. Trips to Paris, Brussels, Amsterdam; celebrations with great friends in Atlanta, New York, New Orleans, Paris again, and then home to Australia and New Zealand. A fun and fulfilling year.

Strange that, in other ways, things were not going so well.

For many years I had this sense of wanting to do something of my own. I didn't know what that something looked like; it was just always in the background. But I was comfortable and trapped in the soft stickiness of that comfort. A nudge from the Universe was required. My previously well-paid and happy career careened off the rails with both the declining fortunes of the company I worked with and the arrival of a new and annoying 'micro-manager.' Although my decision to leave was an emotional response, not a well-thought-out financial one, it was long overdue.

I was surprised by my next move. A chance meeting with a friend led me down a new and winding path. *Really? I'm going to sell insurance?* My limited view of finance was that it was not the creative career I was looking for, but I loved the freedom of being out on my own.

The sense of freedom stayed with me, but the early excitement waned as the disconnect became all too real.

I'm not wearing khaki trousers, but the rest of the world might as well be. I feel organic, rounded at the edges, brightly colored on the inside. My world feels constrained, full of hard angles, the blandest shade of beige, alien. *WTF! How did I end up here?* I feel like my soul is slowly disappearing into a deep, dark hole. Some essential part of me has gone missing.

Beige box, grey world.

This is about the time I find myself in the aisle at Lowes, staring at light bulbs, for what seems like forever. *Do I buy the long-lasting, more expensive one, or the really cheap one?* Despair in my life and chosen career finding an echo in my money and like an echo, reverberating to expand the effect. "Entrepreneur," my friend says, "do you know it literally means 'into being?'" *No kidding?* I'm birthing a new version of Self, and it's painful.

Some women love shoes. I love bags. Learning to appreciate something without needing to buy it was a little tough to begin with. Circling the racks at TJ Maxx, eyes on one particular bag, so cool, so different, wanting it so badly. I remember counseling myself; *It's okay, there will be another one. There is always more to come.*

In hindsight, this was a fabulous experience. It taught me about sufficiency in a very real way. This idea that there was 'enough,' and I could create other ways of bringing fun into my life. I started painting—my Saturday night date—because I loved it and as I already owned the paints, it cost me nothing. I learned how to be practical in my purchases, and most importantly, I began to be aware of and consciously choose how I was spending.

I always tracked my money to a degree, and now I tracked it to the very last cent. Contrary to what you might think, this was a strangely serene activity. I found it grounding, and I found my newfound ability to go without, to not need to buy, buy, buy, liberating. No matter how great the sale, if this one wonderful thing was gone, there would soon be in its place some other wonderful thing. In the western world, at least, we live in a land of plenty. The fear of missing out often drives spending, but, in this over-produced, goods-laden world, you really can't. There is always more to consume.

A good friend gave me sage advice. The question to ask is, not, can I afford this, but does it nurture me? A very different energetic vibration.

Hitting what feels like rock bottom, happily, the only way is up. Walking into my friend's house, a basket in the corner of her kitchen catches my eye, and uncharacteristically I lean down to tidy it. At the very bottom, under the jumbled pile of cookbooks, I discover a different kind of book: one for life. This little book, *Ask and it is Given,* was my introduction to the work of Esther and Jerry Hicks.

I begin to attend the Abraham-Hicks workshops, and the insights gleaned become a pivotal point, a crack of light illuminating the way forward. I start to get coaching and do a huge amount of work on myself energetically, and as I do, I find myself in the company of more and more like-minded souls. I meet artists, writers, coaches, wellness providers, and people who are also wanting to be fully expressed, all the while making a difference in the world. My relationship to my business evolves. I slowly became more of myself, and it becomes more of me until, miraculously, I feel fully congruent with what I do in the world and who I am while doing it. I am my true self, not the version of myself I thought I needed to be, allowing me to thrive and express my own brand of service congruent with both my career and my soul.

Somewhere along the way, I find myself standing in another aisle, this time at Nordstrom's, beguiled by the most beautiful, exotic, colorful, sparkly, and still at the time, quite expensive handbag. This bag I buy. This is my gift to myself and my proof that life is no longer grey.

Discarding old ways of being is a bit like dealing with the bamboo roots snaking through the back of my yard. They have a way of showing up again when the conditions are just right. But I'm persistent. I don't give up, even when that feels like all I want to do. Some of you rule-breakers would have busted out of that beige box a lot sooner and never even experienced what I did, but we all have our journeys, and I've learned a lot about myself on mine.

I'm a continuing and ever-evolving work in progress. I started ballet at 56 and took my first surfing lesson at 57. I plan to do more of both; I see myself surfing those waves and dancing a perfect pirouette. I see myself in that vision that has been with me for as long as I can remember, laughing with family and friends, playing by the water, loved one by my side, with the young girl inside of me laughing with unabashed joy at her most beautiful and fully expressed life.

The Tool

Feeling out of control or unstable regarding money is detrimental to confidence and self-esteem and is not a product of how much money you have. Neither is wealth.

Derived from the old English word "weal," which means "well-being" or "welfare," in our modern world, wealth has come to mean riches of the financial kind. But what about other elements of life that impact our well-being? Good health, satisfaction with our work or career, other skills and attributes we possess that bring joy to ourselves and others? If you haven't already, I'd like to invite you to expand the definition of wealth in your own life.

Also consider that building wealth requires more than just earning money. It's a fact that one can be broke on any income. How you are using, saving, and directing your money also makes a difference.

To be inspired is to be animated or imbued with the spirit to do something. What is the spirit of money for you? What is its purpose? Is your use of and relationship with money fulfilling this purpose?

Steps to creating your own unique version of inspired wealth:

1. Get clear about the purpose of money for you.
2. Create a new and intentional plan for your money.
3. Direct your money according to the purpose you have given it.
4. Have compassion along the way.

Step 1: Get Clear About the Purpose of Money for You.

If you consider the concept of sufficiency, or 'enough-ness,' you most likely have the essentials (a roof over your head and food to eat) taken care of. Anything above this is a choice, and that choice can be intentional, directed, purpose-driven, or simply habitual or accidental.

It will be valuable for you if you can get clear on money's purpose as it can be a useful filter when you need to choose between competing uses for your money.

What makes you happy?

What do you dream of?

Is money for your security or your freedom or both?

How does freedom look to you?

How does security look to you?

What do you care about?

Although the purpose of your money is broader, you can include specific financial goals here.

Note for couples: You may have different values or purposes when it comes to money. This can be a good discussion point when looking at how to allocate surplus cash (after essentials). It's important not to judge each other's perspectives. Our varied backgrounds and experiences mean equally varied ways in which we think about and use money.

Step 2: Create a New and Intentional Plan for Your Money.

You can orchestrate your money with the same care as you plan your vacation, not to restrict yourself, but to support yourself. Because when you're using your money with no plan or pre-thought, the results can be just as random as driving to your vacation destination with no map or GPS and no prior knowledge of the route. You might get lucky, but you might not.

It can be helpful to get clarity around where your money is currently going if you're not already tracking this. Seeing how your money is being currently spent creates the awareness and insight that allows you to redirect that money for your highest benefit.

If you don't want to get this detailed, at the very least, you'll need to know the monthly amount of your essentials and other non-negotiable items. Essentials are generally anything that you must have, for example, food, clothing, home. Non-negotiable items could be core expenses that are not essential but intrinsic to how you live your life or conduct your business. Don't use this as an excuse to ignore these items; this is an opportunity to take an inquiring look at all your expenses. Your remaining cash is surplus, but it should still have an assigned purpose.

When allocating how you are going to use your money, remember to pay yourself first. Make your commitment to savings number one in your payment plan. Be your most important bill rather than waiting to see what is left over at the end of the month. You will be surprised at how well this strategy works. If your income is variable, you can make your savings amount a percentage of your income. As your income increases, increase that percentage. Start with something that you can be consistent with.

Don't avoid savings in favor of debt. Yes, paying high-interest debt is important, but so is having a cash cushion, no matter how small, both psychologically and practically. Cash is Queen!

Be realistic. If you've built up a mountain of debt, it's going to take some effort to bring it back down.

For couples, consider allocating an 'incidentals' or 'whatever I want' category. The idea is that each of you can spend money on something important to you, without any judgment or explanation, because it has already been given to you to do with what you wish. This can be a helpful way to avoid unnecessary money arguments, as can regular money meetings.

Step 3: Direct Your Money According to the Purpose You Have Given It.

This is the fun part!

Spending as an empowered and conscious choice. Voting with your dollars as an expression of what you care about, what's important to you.

If you really want to fine-tune your money relationship, continue to bring awareness to what you are getting in exchange. Is it high on the joy factor? Is it a gift that keeps on giving? Does it take you one step closer to your dream? Yes, I know, it could be a bit time-consuming weighing this up every time you spend. But this awareness will become a habit: spending by design.

To keep yourself on track, separate out your money immediately as the cash comes in. This helps to prevent spending 'creep' based on a bank balance that might be higher than its true value once your money is allocated to its intended purpose. The best way to do this is to physically move the cash into separate accounts for each purpose. These can be as broad or as specific as you need them to be to better manage your money. Many of the online banking options make this an easy thing to do.

If you find yourself overspending, despite your plan, take a closer look at why. Always with curiosity, not judgment.

Step 4: Have Compassion Along the Way.

If money is challenging for you, before dealing with money tasks, take a moment to breathe and center yourself. If possible, go outside, take your shoes off, and plant your feet on the ground. Breathe in the fresh air, feel the sunlight on your face. Throw your arms up, do a silly dance, thank the Universe or God or your personal version of the Divine for the earth's abundance. Money doesn't have to be serious.

If funds are really tight, spend some time noticing all the things you appreciate and love that don't cost you a dime and find your nourishment and joy there. Learn to fill up your happiness tank this way.

Be aware that depriving yourself completely can be like a punishment and may strengthen any money story you have around lack or money worthiness. Allow the occasional treat.

If excess spending is an issue for you, developing this awareness will help you to better check in on whether what you are about to spend money on will truly support you versus an old habit or emotional reaction to something else going on in your life. Great questions to ask when you are about to spend money on anything that is a choice versus a basic need item: "Does this purchase nourish me? Does it support my money purpose?"

Shopping can be like chocolate, something you use when you want to avoid thinking about what's bothering you, when you want to numb or avoid the emotion or mess in your life, work, or relationship. Like chocolate, however, it can result in unwanted pounds in the form of debt, a weight that can be difficult to get rid of and that has a habit of growing exponentially in favor of the credit card companies, not you.

Notice what it is about that shopping experience that makes a difference for you. How does it take your mind off something or act as a happy pill on the days you feel glum? Is it the sense of winning when you find a bargain? Is it seeing something pretty or beautiful (or shiny and new) in your home or wardrobe? If it soothes your soul somehow, even if you can't put your finger on it, ask yourself, *what else has that effect?* For me, I love to get outside. Looking at flowers, my garden, being on the water, walking with a friend, and people watching or bird watching feels peaceful and fills me up in a way that leaves me satisfied, with none of the 'sugar rush or crash' side effects that other habits might entail.

You may not get to everything that needs to be done today, or tomorrow, or even next week. But you will get it done. Lighten up and have some fun along the way and be okay with progressing imperfectly. Have compassion for yourself wherever you may find your Self.

A Final Note

In her book, *Sacred Success*, Barbara Stanny writes, *"…women's resistance to dealing with money has far less to do with the fundamentals of finance than with their fear of (or ambivalence about) power."* She goes on to say, *"Essentially, our fear of power is our fear of becoming who we really are."*

Be inspired. Be wealthy. Be all of who you are and everything you wish to be.

For more on creating your inspired money plan visit **www.heartstrongwealthplanning.com/resources**.

ABOUT THE AUTHOR
Meredith Sims ~ 60

Meredith Sims is an independent Financial Advisor specializing in Financial Planning and Socially Responsible and Impact Investing.

She loves empowering women to step up and take charge of their money, helping them to build a solid financial foundation aligned with their values. Her love of nature and compassion for each living being drives her interest in spending and investing money in a meaningful and earth-friendly way.

As an advisor, Meredith has long been interested in the subject of money from the perspective of conscious connection, using money as a tool and platform to support living a fully expressed life, whatever that may look like for each unique individual—building wealth and building a wealthy life.

A spiritual seeker and artist at heart, Meredith came to Atlanta, GA by way of Perth, Brisbane, London, and Sydney. She believes in the beauty of seeing the individual, the inherent goodness in humanity, and that living a fulfilled, joyful life is a birthright, while not necessarily an immediate destination. She loves getting on a plane and traveling somewhere, has been working on mastering the French language for many years, and no doubt will be for many more. She loves to garden, create, paint, and write, and her happy place is on the water. She has previously written for The Art Section, an online journal of art and cultural commentary.

Meredith can be contacted at **www.heartstrongwealthplanning.com/ contact**.

CHAPTER 15

Mirror, Mirror on the Wall: Reflections After 50

How to See the Beauty Beyond Limitations

By Liz Hanzi, CPCC, ACC, C-IQ Practitioner

Keep looking in the mirror. Not for vanity but for truth. Face it.

—Kimani Fambro

My Story

Exasperated and terrified, I begged, "I can't do this! I can't fly solo! I'm not ready!"

We were side by side in single-engine Cessna Skyhawks.

We took off.

The next thing I knew, I was immersed in the clouds, and my husband's plane was nowhere to be seen. As the clouds dissipated, alarmingly, I saw a mountain directly in front of me! Reacting and swerving quickly to avoid impact, I suddenly found my plane going down. Strangely, it was now nighttime, and I was heading straight into the sea. Moments later, I was surrounded by water, my plane broken into pieces. My arms were holding on desperately to a broken wing of the plane, with the rest of my body dangling in the water. Although I like water, I have a fear of dark waters or being unable to see clearly. I felt the hysteria rise through my body as I realized the abject aloneness, darkness, and fear I felt.

I consciously tried to regulate my breath and not panic. Then, I forced myself to recall the love I had for the sea and how I enjoy swimming. I tried to assure myself that I was safe.

I knew I had to *make* myself okay. I had to go into the darkness, into the water, into the unknown, and be with it all, including the sharks, which I was sure were nearby.

As lucid dreams go, it was then that I realized what I must do. I told myself, *okay, Liz, you know what you need to do. Before you wake up from this dream, you must dive into this dark water, not with fear but with pure joy. You need to make yourself no different than the water itself, no different from marine life. If you come face to face with a shark, it won't recognize you as anything different from itself. You like swimming; you like water, you can do this! Only when you become one with the ocean, one with marine life, and one with the sharks will you be able to wake from this dream.*

I inhaled deeply, held my breath, and dove into the black sea. I dove under with the joy of a child looking for a treasure at the sanded bottom. I kicked, swimming, twisting, and turning, weightless and free. My eyes were wide open; I could see just what was in front of me. Then in the distance, I noticed a beam of rippled light reflecting into the depths from above. I came face to face with a shark, and as I looked into its eyes, we were the same, and it nonchalantly swam away. Then I told myself it was okay to wake up.

I awoke from the dream amazed, alert, transfixed, and awed by the power of it. Smiling, I realized what I had done: I kept my word, I didn't allow myself to wake up until I became 'one with the sea and all life.' Now awakened, I was alone in my bed, feeling at peace, despite my impending divorce.

I remember that dream still 30 years later like it was yesterday though I didn't know at the time what 'lucid' dreaming was. But this isn't about lucid dreaming. This chapter is about being a woman over 50, about taking a good look in the mirror and the various mirrors of our lives, and realizing our fulfillment in life is up to us no matter what limitations or circumstances we may be facing. It's about generating beauty from our own presence, even during hardships, losses, wrinkles, injustices, inequalities, injuries, joys, and triumphs. It's about waking up to the fullness of our lives and learning how to dance in the space between the polarities of right/wrong, good/bad, success/failure, joy/sorrow, and endings and beginnings. This chapter is about how to embrace (and yes, even celebrate) the perceived darkness, the sharks, and the fears, and dare to be happy.

As I approach 60, I have chronic pain and arthritis from injuries and eight major surgeries over the years. Somedays, I feel like a pinball machine wondering what part of my body will light up with pain—seemingly random and without a direct cause. I often wonder, *is this pain from too much sitting, too much walking, too much stretching, too much worry or negativity, too many inflammatory foods, or not enough water? Will ice or heat help, or should I take meds, increase my meditation practice? Do I use the cervical traction device, hang from my inversion table, or rest today?* Ugh! It can be maddening!

As you could guess, my physical activity is severely limited. It was a wake-up call to realize how much my well-being and identity were linked to my physicality. Strenuous exercise kept my depression at bay; it helped activate my mind and contributed to my sense of purpose by living an active life of teaching, coaching, and training. I found I was also attached to the feeling and appearance of being physically fit. I know that how we look and feel in our physical body, what our health is like and how pain cycles work, are directly related to our perceptions and mindset, as well as to the levels of fulfillment we have in all areas of our lives. I try to take in the whole picture when assessing my pain. In the last several years, I also noticed I was waking up to other parts of my life that felt limiting or painful.

Physical pain has a way of demanding our attention, while other pain can be more subtle. Other wake-up calls presenting as pain, for example, showed up when my boys left home. I experienced a deep sense of loss around my purpose and identity, despite my career. I also noticed feeling more limited when I recognized that my husband and I had not achieved the financial security we wanted. These shortcomings also showed up in my environment as my house called out in need of repairs and improvements. I was also deeply pained when I saw how one son flourished, and the other struggled with some of the genetic deficiencies I passed along. All these wake-up calls reflected my perceived limitations, exacerbated by social media which naturally tempts us to compare our insides to other people's outsides.

Although I thought my pain, limitations, and circumstances were unique, what I have noticed—as a woman over 50—is that so many others also wake up to feelings or circumstances that elicit pain, disappointment, or inadequacies. It's natural at this age to look at and reflect on most, if not *all*, areas of our lives. So, when the Snow White analogy came to my mind and asked:

'Mirror, mirror on the wall, who's the fairest
(most successful-healthiest-happiest-with the pretty home-great relationships-suc-
cessful kids)
of them all?'

My own mirror reflected and answered with, "Certainly not you."

Looking back, it almost seemed 'easy' to take on one big heart-wrenching transition, such as a divorce. It helped to have that lucid dream. It gave me hope and inspiration and encouraged me to get through a really difficult time. But at almost 60, with the mirror reflecting so many different apparent limitations, it's been challenging to say, "Dive in, face your fears!" This time it's not just dark water invoking fear, preventing me from seeing clearly, or one shark that I need to make peace with. This time it feels like a whole host of perceived dangers, disappointments, and feelings of inadequacy that seem to be lurking below the surface, along with my overriding chronic pain. The mirror on the wall didn't just reflect my physical image but showed me all I've created in the various areas and relationships of my life: the good, the bad, and the ugly.

Now, my judge wants to shame, belittle, and discount my feelings with phrases like, *Oh, things could be much worse!* And, *be grateful for what you have!* Which are undeniably true statements and are helpful at times, but overall not very productive.

It takes more than a 'think positive' mindset or any of the various spiritual bypassing we can do to meditate, pray, or affirm ourselves into a transformed state. I can't tap away my pain or limiting beliefs. These are great tools and are very useful at times, yet even those can act as an escape to cover up or bypass our pain. Our pain, limitations, and saboteurs are still waiting for us to meet them. Like my lucid dream, for any of our limitations or fears, we must come eye-to-eye with them and see them not for the predators they appear to be but as an integral part of who we

Wholehearted Wonder Women 50 PLUS

are, deserving of respect and love. Only if we're willing to dive in, dare to playfully engage them and merge with them, will they cease to have power over us. Only then can the bad, the ugly, the dark and scary, even the pain, become beautiful.

Beauty is the ability to see and accept myself as I am, not how I think I should be. The same is true for my circumstances. I need to first look in the mirror and radically accept where I am. This is not a surrender-type-of-acceptance but a radically empowered acceptance. An overly simplified way of looking at this is, "It is what it is, or I am that I am...now what?"

A favorite meditation of mine ends with, "Invite all parts of yourself to the peace table in your heart." This may feel counterintuitive. After all, we don't want to feed or give too much energy to our saboteurs, fears, or pain, yet they are undeniably a part of life. So, one way to do that is by inviting them in. We can all swim or sit together at the table. However, by recently recalling my dream, the one thing I've never truly done is to *celebrate* them.

I was taught in my coaching training to celebrate failures. It sounded good, and I believed in the concept and believed it for other people. But I couldn't authentically celebrate my pain, failures, or what I disliked about myself! Especially with the additional and newly-presented over-50 limitations I felt deep down inside. I wilted in complete overwhelm. I needed something radical!

Like my profound lucid dream when I was a wise 29-year-old, now more than ever, I realized I had to dive in joyfully! Not just past tense, I have to, over and over again, practice embracing the joys of swimming with all parts of myself. I swim with the depths of my feelings, my pain, and all the stories of my life. I feel my weightless body at peace with whatever comes my way. This allows me to acknowledge my humanness and oneness with all life, especially in pain, fear, and worry.

I am not just the content of my life acquired over decades of living. I'm not just validated by the 'good' titles and roles, accomplishments, appearances, and accumulation of wealth. I saw that the mirrors in my life reflected the sum of my experiences, and I had to look beyond the surface reflections and welcome *all* the different perceptions I had. I had to become willing to take responsibility for them. I had to focus on and become the context by which all content is allowed to even exist. I had to become one with it all, and the crazy part is, in celebration.

This may all sound a bit outlandish. But here's what's true: we have a choice. If we can be more aware of our fears and the source of our suffering, we can choose to dive in and swim with them to celebrate our humanness AND our divine connection. Or we can also choose to be with our pain, with loss or grief, without trying to change it or fix it. We can make room for it, be present, and sit with it with compassion. But we can't stay there forever. Still, either choice is a conscious one, and each can be really beautiful.

So, how do we see the beauty beyond limitations? How do we feel beautiful (and dare to celebrate) when we're suffering? How do we have the willingness to see the beauty—and the possibility of it—in the mirror with whatever is presented to us? We do this by celebrating how clever and powerful we are, both in what we manifest by way of our saboteurs and what we manifest through our clearly proud and easily worn successes. We get to practice celebrating the energy source or life force inherent in and behind pain, fear, limitation, pleasure, excitement, and success. And the more we practice it, the more the neuroplasticity of our brains responds by reorganizing our old patterns of suffering. If we give up the resistance to pain, we create more openness. When we celebrate the energy source of life itself, we open ourselves up to more and more possibilities and miracles.

We end up suffering less, and we celebrate more our own autonomy over this crazy, wild, trippy ride we call life!

I invite you to dare to dive deep, swim with delight, and see the beauty within and beyond any limitations!

The Tool

Reflection and Redirection

(You can use the two parts of this tool separately or together)

Part I. Deliberate Seeing and Journaling Through Self-Reflection

What if looking in the mirror was genuinely loving, amazing (in an awe-struck kind of way), beautiful and reverent - even for the messy, imperfect, and nasty parts?

Set a timer for five minutes. Gaze at yourself, your eyes, your face, or even your whole body in a mirror (preferably without make-up or clothes).

Go beyond the reflection and look deeper inside to touch your humanity. Swim with all the imperfections. Look at the power you have to create and be with all sorts of different experiences. What would it look like to celebrate the dark times, the pain, or the limitations? What would it be like to look at the parts you don't like, and like the shark in my dream, meet it with equanimity, connecting yourself to the energy or life source, where there is no separation between right/wrong, good/bad, ugly or beautiful?

Write about how it felt to celebrate ALL of it, all of the energy that is you. What was it like to look into your eyes and explore yourself with non-judgmental curiosity and possibility?

Part II. Redirection Through Meditation

This tool is great for those of us who find it easier at times to help others but can often overlook ourselves. This meditation is based on the Buddhist practice of Tonglen, which awakens our heart and our compassion.

1. Sit in a comfortable place, take two full breaths to let your body and mind soften and open.

2. For the next several breaths, focus on visualizing a texture, color, or sensation of each in-breath and each out-breath.

For the Inhale, visualize what pain or suffering feels and looks like to you. So, it might be a tangly, webbed, sticky, dark substance, or a hot, red, fiery, lava-type sensation, or maybe it's more like a dark, cloudy, heavy-laden feeling.

For the exhale, visualize a cool, light, and breezy sensation, or a green, nourishing, luscious feeling, or maybe a fluid, sparkly, dancing light sensation.

3. Now, take your personal situation, any fear, worry, anger, pain, suffering, feelings of inadequacy or shame, and think of all the people around the globe who have those same feelings at times. See the nameless, countless others who right now might be feeling a very similar feeling.

4. Breathe in that pained feeling for yourself and others. Attach whatever color, visualization, or sensation that comes to mind to describe that feeling.

5. Breathe out whatever comes to mind to describe the opposite of that pain like lightness of being, fluidity, freedom, exhaling out confidence, strength, or success.

6. Continue to breathe in the described pain for yourself and all others who know this pain and exhale out the relief and serenity you wish for yourself and all others for as long as you wish.

For variation, sometimes, I will start this practice first with me and my pain. Then, I open it to include other people in my neighborhood who might be feeling this way. (I don't need to see their faces or know them). Then, the next breath includes people in my city, then the whole state, expanding out in the next breath to the continent, across the globe, and even to the atmosphere for any lingering pain or suffering in the air.

7. Before ending this meditation, let your breath relax (here I like to then put my hands in prayer position in front of my heart and bow my head gently) and take a moment to acknowledge yourself for taking the time to do this for yourself, others, and for the world. Visualize yourself wrapped in a blanket of compassion (I usually choose a color) and before you open your eyes, curve your mouth into a little smile. This will signal your brain that this is something you enjoy and will feel good about doing again.

I would love to hear about your experience with these tools! Sign up for my free gift: Manifesting Midlife Mojo - How to Defeat Anxiety in Five Simple Steps, to hear more about my programs, or to reach out for a free consult at **www.livinglifecomplete.com**.

ABOUT THE AUTHOR
Liz Hanzi ~ 60

Liz Hanzi, owner of Living Life Complete Professional Coaching, is a Midlife Specialist/Professional Life-Leadership Coach, Teacher, and Author. She is a Certified Professional Co-Active Coach, a Core Practitioner of CI-Q (Conversational Intelligence Quotient), and a Certified Coach by the International Coach Federation with over 12 years and 1000's of hours of coaching experience. With a degree in Philosophy and years incorporating and teaching health, wellness, and mindfulness practices, she specializes in guiding busy, professional women through the uncertainty in Midlife transitions using cutting edge approaches in coaching, philosophy, and neuroscience to deepen their self-knowledge, to strengthen their self-acceptance and personal responsibility, and to help them express themselves in a more integrated and soulful way. She listens and engages her clients to identify their vision and expand opportunities through heightened self-care and mindset development, targeted action, self-leadership, and trusting, effective communication.

The result is confident and empowered women who are healthier, more serene, more productive and effective in all their relationships.

She has been featured on Atlanta Interfaith Broadcasting, covering topics on "Handling Stress in Everyday Life," "How to be the CEO of Your Life," and "How to Cultivate Resiliency in Midlife." She also has volunteered her coaching services to the Humanitarian Coaching Network as well to C4E - Coaching 4 Educators - a global nonprofit company whose mission is to offer coaching to teachers all over the world.

Her professional services include 1:1 Professional Coaching, Conversational Leadership Programs, Lifestyle Health Assessments, and her Program: The 3 Pillars to End the Suffering of Uncertainty and Create a Life You Love: A Course In Re-Awakening at Midlife.

Feel free to reach out and connect at:

www.livinglifecomplete.com

https://twitter.com/lhanzi

https://instagram.com/LizHanzi

http://www.linkedin.com/in/LizHanzi

CHAPTER 16

Dare to Embark on the Journey You Fear Most

Recovering from Rape and Depression, Moving Forward in Love

By Bridgette Graham-Barlow, CHT, RMT, CST, MT, Spiritual and Life Coach, The Yuen Method

"Yes, I'm wise, but it's wisdom born of pain."
—Helen Reddy

My Story

The trip of a lifetime was the trip that changed my life forever.

It's early morning and the sky has a thick gloomy overcast as Rachel and I pack and prepare to leave for the airport near Red Square, Moscow. This was the second leg of the four it takes to get home. There's still snow and ice on the ground, much of it dirty from the city traffic. We drove past Saint Basil's Cathedral, one of the oldest and well-known landmarks in

Europe. I love history and the stories of the human experience. Originally, I wanted to tour it all on this trip, but now all I want to do is to get the hell out of this godforsaken, barbaric country.

The three of us (Rachel, myself and our boss, Harry, now known to us as a heartless evil man) were dropped off at the airport. Rachel was pregnant and it was a difficult two-week trip for her. She suffered from morning sickness throughout the day. I felt bad for her but was accustomed to her frequent bouts of nausea. This trip was supposed to be the most exciting trip of our lives and nothing was going to stop us. The song, *I am Woman*, from Helen Reddy played daily in my head as my motivating theme song in the planning of this trip. Here we are, two American women in 1990 on a business trip to renovate a well-known healing center hidden in the mountains of Soviet Georgia.

Wow, we had *arrived*! We were breaking some glass ceilings out there and helping women move forward. I remember feeling filled with brilliant ideas, feeling strong and invincible! Yes, I was on top of the world at 29. This opportunity was exciting and one we had worked hard to get our company to take. We worked for a very large land development company in the Washington, DC area. Rachel was a fire protection engineer and also handled the marketing until the company hired me. *A dream job for me,* or so I thought at the time.

I loved marketing, my mind was quick and willing to learn and grow. Meeting with clients and helping them was what I did well. In this industry there were so many possibilities. Rachel and I were friends since we were five and had a great time working together side by side. This trip was a huge deal for our future and a feather in our cap. This was going to help our company go international and it was because of us. But now I was no longer filled with this joy and enthusiastic spirit.

Rachel and I checked in at the airport gate and went to grab a quick bite. I could barely eat. I was scared and in shock over the events that happened two nights ago. But nothing was going to stop me from leaving this awful, depressive, and oppressed country. A place where women were treated as property, abused, and had no rights. My focus was to do whatever it took to get home to my son. I knew better than to stir the pot and send up any red flags. I needed to remain calm and act as if nothing happened. I thought, *just don't bring any attention to yourself.* I knew the powers that I was in contact with had a very high-ranking position in the government. This man had the power to make me disappear. We were made aware early on in the trip by our bodyguards and interpreter—provided for us by the Soviet government—of the sale of women on the black market. They said women like us, particularly me because Rachel was pregnant, could bring a pretty penny. I remember thinking I had heard of the sex slave business but I really didn't know it existed. It was hard to believe I found myself in this situation. The threat was real.

As we sat and ate our food, we overheard two men at the counter ordering and realized they were Americans! It was almost two weeks since we had met or spoken to an American. It's funny how when you travel abroad you can tell the American accent regardless of where they live in the US. Rachel and I quickly introduced ourselves to the two business-men. The conversation felt so comforting and for a few minutes I felt safe. We discovered they were also there on a business trip and had been there several times. One was from Chicago and jolly in nature, and the other soft-spoken gentleman was from New York City.

We found out they were taking the same flight, which made me feel even better. These complete strangers were the first men we had encountered in the last two weeks who treated us with kindness and respect. I don't know how it happened, but Rachel and I found ourselves telling them that I had been raped by a high-ranking government official and was afraid to talk about it for fear of being sold or worse, killed. We explained how the trip was difficult on so many levels for us. They were shocked and appalled to learn we approached our boss several times and asked for his help from the very beginning. I explained the last time I talked with my boss that he became angry and said to me, "You are naive and unworldly. Don't fuck up this deal." From the moment I arrived, the men holding lower-level government positions made sexual comments or innuendos toward me. You'd think they had never seen a woman or blonde in their life.

In fact, the first night I arrived one said, "Me Tarzan, you Jane," and insisted I take a drink from him. I politely declined and thought his insistence was very suspicious. From that moment on I felt uneasy and their comments only worsened as the days continued. The only reprieve was when a higher up official was introduced to the group and all other advances toward me stopped. Then and only then did I begin to feel better and safe. Little did I know this was because he marked me as his.

We all finished our food and made our way to the airplane, boarded and took our seats. Our new friends were in first class and we were in business class. Rachel sat next to our boss so I didn't have to. Thank goodness. Just the mere presence of him made me sick and upset. As we settled in our seats and waited for takeoff our boss ignored us and read the financial page of the newspaper. The plane began to move down the runway and we heard the wheels lift. Suddenly, I began to shake and cry. It was like the flood gates opened and I couldn't stop myself. I hadn't permitted myself to show or feel any emotion until that moment for fear we would never get out of there. At that very moment I felt relief and thought *they can't get me. They can't hurt me or sell me.* We were no longer on USSR soil. Rachel held me as I quietly wept and our boss continued to read the newspaper.

Now you know why we called him a heartless, evil man. We never saw that side of him before.

Shortly after liftoff, Jeff, the man from Chicago, walked back to check on us. He saw Rachel holding me while we both wept, and our boss reading his paper and it upset him. He talked to us for a moment and left. He came back a few minutes later and told us there were seats in first class and he had arranged to have us moved there. We couldn't believe our ears and hurriedly gathered our things and found our seats next to our new friends and protectors. As we flew, I discovered Jeff was a funny man and reminded me of the comedian Rodney Dangerfield in *Caddyshack* and Tom, from New York City, was married with a wife who worked as a rape crisis counselor. Wow, what are the chances of that? These two beautiful souls tried so hard to keep us smiling and laughing the entire trip back. I was certain we had met angels.

We landed, exchanged numbers, and said our goodbyes in New York. Rachel and I boarded another plane home to DC where my parents and Rachel's husband Ron meet us at the airport. I told my parents Rachel and I had to go over some business details and I'd see them tomorrow. The truth was I was feeling shaky, depressed, and wasn't ready to tell my parents what happened. I needed the night to regroup. Rachel told her husband what happened to me and they took me to the hospital to get checked out.

The local hospital was about to turn me away because the rape didn't happen in their county when Ron stepped in and threatened them with going to the newspapers and news stations. He said he would tell them that the hospital turned away a rape victim. That was the first time I heard someone call me a *rape victim*. Those words continued to echo in my ears. I felt weak, sad, and mostly numb. I realized then I felt oddly empty, like a shell of a person. The hospital decided to check me in and do a rape kit on me. I laid there on the cold table. As they examined me, tears streaming down my face, I felt like I was being assaulted again. It was awful, degrading, and humiliating to relive that moment. I felt deeply scarred. Shortly after that, the test results came back. The Soviet official had given me gonorrhea! I couldn't believe it. I've never had any issues of that sort in my entire life. I felt dirty. Fortunately, I was told it was successfully treatable by medicine.

Five weeks later I found out I was pregnant. This was unbearable! I couldn't get this horrendous event out of my life quick enough. It's very hard to heal when something keeps coming up to remind me of that night. I let my boss know I might need additional medical and psychological help to get through this. I was hoping my insurance covered that at the very least. Shortly after, I terminated the pregnancy.

Two weeks later the company served me with legal papers. I was accused of going to the USSR with the intent to create discord among the Soviets and the Americans. They placed a gag order on me. My head was spinning. Hell, there was no need for a gag order, I didn't want to tell anybody this story. I needed help to get through it. Some might ask, "why are you still working for that monster?" I was a single mom making the best money I ever made. But now I felt mentally weak and lost all confidence. I was doing the best I could to keep it together and just wanted this to all go away.

On top of all this mayhem, I was forced to find an attorney to represent me. I talked with four attorneys and at first each one was chomping at the bit for this case but then realized my boss' political ties and dropped me. Two attorneys came on to me. It was disgusting. You could tell they were turned on by the details of the rape! Fortunately, at some point Rachel and I went to the EEOC and filed a complaint against the company which had nothing to do with this case. It had to do with several sexist comments made to Rachel by our boss. The company could not fire us since they were being investigated.

Here is where the angels come in again. Jeff gave me a call one day and asked how I was doing. I explained the mess I was in and he said, "Let me check on something and I'll get back to you." Thirty minutes later he called back and said, "Okay kiddo I found you an attorney. Have you heard of Melvin Belli?" I said no. Jeff said, "He is a well-known national attorney with firms all over the country and he has a firm in the DC area too." I couldn't believe my ears. Turns out the firm was within a half a mile from my house!

There were many meetings with the attorney and many days I thought I wouldn't make it. It took months. I suffered from night terrors, with episodes of screaming and intense fear. In my dreams people were chasing me and I couldn't get away. I began sleepwalking so I made sure I went to bed in street clothes. I sought the help of several therapists until I felt they had no more tools to teach me. I finally ended up in a deep depression. I was diagnosed with clinical depression and placed on medicine for fear I would take my own life. I didn't want to kill myself. I just didn't want to live feeling like this anymore.

Over the next year we battled the company and I got sicker. We won our lawsuit out of court, with a good pay-out. During that time, I became completely debilitated and worn down. I could no longer hide my depression. My family found out and intervened. Arrangements were made to have me and my son move to Virginia Beach, where we lived with my parents so I could heal. My mom grew concerned that I was not getting better, and with her insistence, I found something to do to help. I enrolled in the Edgar Cayce School of Massage Therapy. This was the start of my journey with natural healing.

I spent several years taking courses to better myself and learned I was a natural intuitive and compassionate healer. This gave me great pleasure and purpose. As time went on, I decided I would call myself a healing facilitator. All people have the ability to heal themselves; they just need a healing facilitator to quicken the process.

Now that I'm healed and have neutralized the events that caused my depression, I can move forward in love and see the many beautiful and even enjoyable moments of our trip. I no longer feel victimized by the rape. In this journey I discovered my true path as an intuitive healer and healing facilitator.

The Tool

As a Life and Spiritual Coach, I use many tools to help my clients. Below is one you may try for yourself to help with releasing stored trauma.

Trauma release exercises (TRE) are exercises designed to invoke neurogenic tremors to release chronic muscular tension held within the body. The main muscle that we focus on is the psoas, which is the gravitational center of the body.

The first few exercises stretch hip and leg muscles. Then while lying down on the back, with feet together and legs apart, most of the shaking will take place.

1. Stand with your feet hip-width apart. Roll your feet onto the outer edge of one foot and inner edge of the other foot. Put all your weight equally on both feet. Then roll your feet to the other side. Repeat 10x on each side.

2. Stand with one foot forward, put your full weight on that foot, using the foot behind for balance. Raise your toes, let your back foot leave the ground. Stand on the front toes for a few minutes. You can use a chair or table to help you balance. Repeat 10x on each foot.

3. Stand on one foot, bend the other knee behind you in the air. Put both hands down on the ground, on either side of the foot for balance. Bend and straighten the leg that you are standing on. Repeat 10x on both legs.

4. Stretch your feet wide apart. Put your fists on the small of your back. Bend knees, push your pelvis forward and lean your head back and breathe. Repeat three times.

5. Straighten up then turn and look as far as you can over your shoulder and breathe (legs still apart, hands still on back). Change and look over the other shoulder. Repeat 3x for each side. With legs wide apart bend forward, stretch your arms out with your fingers touching the floor. Bend one knee and walk your hands to that foot and breathe. Bend the other knee and do the same. Repeat three times for each foot.

6. Shake the body out. Stand with your back against the wall, feet apart, and bend your knees, you should be able to see your toes. Rest your hands against your sides for five minutes.

7. Lie on the floor, push the soles of your feet together, legs apart. Lift pelvis about two centimeters off the ground and hold five minutes or for as long as you can without pain.

Drop pelvis, with soles of your feet touching, lift knees five centimeters off the ground for five minutes, then ten centimeters for five minutes and finally, fifteen centimeters for five minutes. Rest.

The tremors vary from person to person. You may feel a lot of trembling or barely feel a thing. The more you do it the more the trembling will spread starting in your legs and hips, moving to your stomach, then chest and head.

TRE was developed by Dr Berceli for PTSD. He found that it could be used as a relief from stresses, anxiety, and depression.

Bridgette Graham-Barlow ~ 60

Bridgette Graham-Barlow, known as Bella to most, is the CEO of Healing Concepts, located in Virginia Beach, Virginia for the past 20 years. Her center won the 2020 Gold Award from Coastal Virgina Magazine for Best Alternative Health Center and offers many healing modalities to help her clients.

She embodies the very meaning of holistic health. Her passion is to teach people what it means to have a mind-body-spirit connection. She is a deeply compassionate person with the desire and commitment to help her clients find the root cause of their trauma, and provide tools to help them heal, grow, and thrive.

Her open and honest communication style help clients feel comfortable and safe immediately. She loves teaching her clients to shift how they see an event, ultimately shifting their experience of that event and helping them peel away the layers one by one.

As a Life and Spiritual Coach, she uses many tools to help access healing. Her training as a Hypnotist, Reiki Master and teacher, Craniosacral therapist, and Yuen Method practitioner have assisted thousands of people to shift their experiences away from trauma and pain - away from feeling the victim to becoming the victor.

Bridgette is a lifelong learner and passionate about helping people reach their full potential. Her innate and intuitive abilities are an added bonus to her clients.

She is recently married, is a mother and grandmother; an artist and photographer; lover of animals, and an avid organic gardener. She enjoys cooking for her friends and family, loves Italy and looks forward to finishing her book!

You can connect with Bridgette at:

Website: **www.healingconceptsnow.com**

Facebook: **https://www.facebook.com/healingconceptsnow**

Email: **Healingconceptsnow@gmail.com**

CHAPTER 17

Tame The Flame

Transforming Anger & Resentment to Love & Connection

By Corinne Coppola, M.A., Founder - CONQUER the Invisible

"Forgive others, not because they deserve forgiveness, but because you deserve peace."
—Jonathan Huie

My Story

Yes, I've been there. Betrayal—we all have experienced it, in one form or another. We have either been deceived by someone or have deceived someone else, or even worse, deceived ourselves. We do it ALL of the time. The truth is hard, but what is harder is living with the lie that either we or someone else has created. Then, we find ourselves living a life where our outsides do not match our insides. You know what I mean: to everyone else, it looks like we have everything we need— a lovely home, beautiful family, friends, vacations, career, cars—everything that society defines as success. But on the inside, you're absolutely miserable. You argue with your partner/spouse/children; you feel lonely and disconnected from your friends, you feel depressed and anxious about your future and the future of your family, and on and on and on.

There are the big "B" betrayals and the small "b" betrayals.

Some examples of big betrayals:
- Emotional, physical and sexual abuse.
- Sexual and emotional intimacy violations in relationships.
- Friend "break-ups."
- Being fired for "no apparent reason."
- Being lied to by a trusted friend or family member.

Some examples of small betrayals:
- Not being honest with ourselves about our feelings in a relationship.
- Doing things to please family and friends to "keep the peace."
- Making a commitment to yourself or someone else and not following through.
- Continuing to work in a job or career you hate, but you need a paycheck.
- Staying in a relationship or friendship too long.

And how many times do the small "b" betrayals become the big "B" betrayals? As an adult, almost 100% of the time. We ignore the signs the body gives us. Anxiety, doubt, confusion, or uneasiness arise as a pit in the stomach, tension in the shoulders, heart racing, sweaty palms, etc. Or maybe it's a question we ask someone that is rhetorical, but they affirm the answer we want to hear, so we disregard the red flag. When these signs are present, it's always a "No" or "Not Yet" or "Not Ready." However, these signs are often pushed aside because we *think* we *know* what's best when our body tells us otherwise.

It's like from the show *Lost In Space* where the robot says, "DANGER Will Robinson! DANGER!" and we shrug it off and keep going. It was having my best friend rage at another friend and having her declare, "I'll never do that to you," only for it to happen to me, a few months later. And the aftermath is me curled up in a ball, in my bed, in utter disbelief and feeling shame, having not listened to the "Danger Will Robinson! Danger!" voice. I'm riddled with the, *why me? I should have seen it coming; I should have known better.* And none of it serves me or my healing. You know what I'm talking about; you've been there.

It's happened to me so many times; friendships, intimate relationships, family relationships, professional situations, etc. I could go on and on. And the story I tell myself is that these people are bad, untrustworthy, and deceitful, and the seeds of anger, doubt, uncertainty, and fear are planted in my heart. These seeds soon blossom into beliefs that I'm unlovable, unworthy, and not good enough, and feelings of shame, guilt, and power-lessness start to take root. Hence, the tree of victimhood begins to grow, and anger and resentment are the lenses through which I view my most important relationships. *I will never get hurt again the way that (so and so) hurt me. I will protect myself at all costs. No one will ever get close enough.*

So how do we stop this cycle of betrayal and dishonesty and tame the flame of anger and resentment that typically ensues and transform it into love and connection?

Get ready. I'm going to use the "F" word. Not the four-letter F word, but the loving "F" word: FORGIVENESS. So before you say, "I know, I know, I know, I've tried, and it just doesn't work for me," let me share a bit of my story.

For me, my journey of betrayal and forgiveness began in May 2007. My husband had a business trip to Hawaii, and we were thrilled to add four nights in Hana, Maui. It was dreamy and romantic and all the things you would imagine a trip to Hawaii would be. We drove the famed Road to Hana in a convertible; the smells were magnificent and unlike anything I had ever experienced. Little did I know that in just over 72 hours, my life would change forever.

I had a Watsu massage the day before we were planning to leave. It was truly a unique opportunity, as this type of massage is not found on the East Coast where I lived. You're submerged in water while the massage therapist puts pressure on specific points in your body to encourage release. And RELEASE I did. The massage therapist, who looked like Jesus by the way, said to me, "Give me whatever you need to; I can hold it."

The next morning, during sexual intimacy with my husband, body memories of incest came flooding back; incest by my father. I was dazed and confused, overwhelmed and in shock; my whole world was shattered. My then-husband believed he caused irreparable harm through an intimate, pleasurable act. The shame, embarrassment, confusion, disbelief, and rage were swarming us both. In that moment, little did I know that it would launch me into a path of awakening I could never have planned for.

I was desperate for answers: *How could this be true? How could my mother let this happen? How could he do this to me and live with himself?* It began an unraveling of my life for which I was unprepared and certainly ill-equipped. When I spoke my truth to a few chosen family members, I was rejected and thought to be a liar. Ties were severed with my family and close family friends. I confronted my father in a therapy session with the intention and hope for healing to begin. His response was, "I don't recollect."

With that, my decision was clear. Any healing I did was going to be mine; there would be no reconciliation. I was determined to heal for my children and for my children's children. When this truth was revealed, there were very few opportunities for support, as it was long before the #MeToo movement. I lost what I thought was my foundation of unconditional love and acceptance and had no physical loss to speak of.

I didn't know then what was waiting for me down the pike.

It was a warm, clear evening in June 2014. I came home from teaching a yoga class, and my husband's car was parked out front, but he did not answer when I called out for him. On the inside, my heart started pounding out of my chest as I recalled my husband's distant and short-tempered behavior over the past few weeks. I checked for his car again, and it was gone. So I called him, "Hey there, where are you?" I said with curiosity and confusion as he picked up the phone. "Your car was out front when I pulled up to the house tonight. And just a few minutes later, you were gone." "Oh, I'm just running to CVS to pick something up. I'll be back soon," he responded. "Okay," I said as I hung up the phone and shrugged. As I turned around, I saw his wallet lying on the counter. I froze, and the hair on the back of my neck stood up as I instantly knew he was lying again. I called a dear friend who lived a few houses down from me and left a message, "S is lying again. I'm done." My husband and I separated a few years earlier for nine months due to infidelities and lies. I thought we had recovered. Apparently not.

About 30 minutes later, my husband came through the door, and I met him in the hallway with his wallet. With a very measured voice, I said, "If you have any respect for me and the 22 years we have been together, you will tell me the truth." He paused for a moment, our eyes locked, and he said, "I don't want to be married anymore. I'm addicted to porn, and I'm seeing M." The truth was finally out.

In that moment, I was full of rage, disgust, hurt, wrath, and fury. The feelings of betrayal and anger would fester over several years as we navigated the divorce. Many times over the years, I played the role of the victim, and I played it well. The unraveling of the marriage began several years before when the truth of my childhood surfaced. I was angry at the world, and it was no surprise that the lies and betrayals of my childhood were carried into my most significant relationship in adulthood. I married a man that continued the same patterning I experienced in my childhood. Secrets, lies, and betrayals. Was this the legacy I would pass down to my children?

At the time, these events were life-shattering; I did not see the gift in any of them. I only saw betrayal, deceit, dishonesty, and lies. The wounds were deep, and I thought I would never be able to recover or regain a sense of myself in the world. I was riddled with loss, grief, rage, shame, disbelief, overall emotional and spiritual devastation. The story I told myself about how I was treated and tossed aside by my family and friends fed directly into, *it's not my fault. They are to blame. They are liars, manipulators and are cowardly and weak.* After all, I was a little girl when the abuse started. It was not my fault. It's true that what happened was not my fault *and* the healing from it *is my* responsibility.

I did it all—talk therapy, exercise, gratitude practice, prayer, yoga, journaling, meditation, energy healings, nature walks, intuitives, bodywork, etc. There was no roadmap to my healing. Deep shame, guilt, humiliation, and an overall feeling of disgrace helped reinforce the stigma and silence I experienced. The truth is I was quite comfortable in my victim role. The shame, fear, doubt, self-loathing, and rage all suited me. Several professionals and friends had suggested I try to find a way to forgiveness. I had heard it all:

"Resentment is like drinking poison and waiting for the other person to get sick."

"Forgiveness is letting go of the hope that the past will be different."

"Forgiveness is not about letting the other person off the hook. It's about your own freedom."

"Forgiveness is a gift you give yourself."

Until I began to see the chaos being created in all of my relationships as a result of my holding on to the rage and resentment from what was done to me, I was not ready to change. I thought I had forgiven and "moved on," but in truth, I hadn't. The rage and resentment were always lingering in the backdrop of my life. The insanity was spilling over to my most important relationships and hurting people I loved the most.

A turning point came one day on a walk with my children in Spring 2020. Easter passed, and I didn't receive flowers from my children as I had asked. I thought I would gently address the oversight and make a loving request. What I received in return was a firm yet cutting response from one of them, "Mom, when will you believe that I love you?" It absolutely took my breath away. WOW. It was a moment of realization I needed to change the way I was showing up in my relationships.

And so, my real journey towards forgiveness began. Almost 13 years after my memories came back and almost six years since my marriage ended, I started to take the first steps in *real* forgiveness and in letting go of the anger, rage, and resentment that festered in me for years. If I wanted authentic love and connection, I needed to *truly* let go and forgive myself for the rage and resentment I held on to for so long.

The Tool

Forgiveness = Love and Connection

First, I want to remind you that **forgiveness IS a process** and there is no timeline. It is similar to grief. Forgiveness, like grief, is a cyclical process. And it's a process you need to feel your way through. Reminiscent of the children's story, *We Are Going On A Bear Hunt*, "We can't go over it, we can't go under it, we have to go through it." Yes, you are going to have to feel those feelings.

Secondly, **forgiveness is a decision**. Even having the desire to have the intention to forgive is a decision towards forgiveness. You need to **decide** if the person who injured you will continue to be in control of your life or are *you* going to be in control of your life? By continuing to be in the story of anger, hate, rage, and resentment, you allow the other person to be in control and continue to steal your joy and freedom. Every time you blame the person who hurt you, you give away your power.

Third, **in any moment, you can begin again**. You do not have control over a trigger (person, place, or thing), but you do have control over *how* you respond.

Finally, above all else, **we need to have forgiveness for ourselves** which begins with self-compassion. Let's do this together, so you can see how it works. Start slowly and use a situation or person that you have experienced a minor falling-out. Any forgiveness work caused by a traumatic event should be done in the presence and care of a qualified professional.

1. Begin by finding a comfortable place to sit or lie down. Close your eyes or cast them down and take a few deep breaths, in through the nose and exhaling out of the mouth with an audible sigh. Let everything else go and come to the present moment. If you are able, notice your feet and wiggle your toes. Use any of your senses to bring you to the present moment.

2. Bring the person or situation to mind that hurt you. Visualize the person in as much detail as possible—time of day, what you are wearing, facial expressions, tone, etc.

3. Set the intention to forgive.

You may want to stop here and just notice the sounds around you or the rhythm of your breath or a neutral spot on your body, like your elbow, and gently rest. There is no need to go any further.

If there is any area of tension or holding, send the breath to that area to encourage it to release. *Do not* force it. If your body is not ready to soften, it is telling you, you're not ready, and you need to listen. Be gentle with yourself. Stop where you are, acknowledge what you're feeling, place a hand on your heart and say to yourself, "Of course I feel this way." You've come a long way just by being willing to consider an intention to forgive.

If you are able to move on, go to Step 4.

4. When a difficult emotion arises, we can use a process called **RAIN**.

Recognize what is happening. Notice what you are experiencing. If possible, allow it to surface. What are the physical sensations? Is there an image or shape or size, or color? If possible, Name the emotion.

Allow the difficult feelings, thoughts, or experiences to be there. We tend to shut down or numb out when challenging things arise. We will avoid at all costs, but what we resist persists and comes back stronger. If you can take a moment, pause, and give yourself space to really be in your experience, you will have more understanding of what is actually going on.

Investigate. Can you become curious about your experience - what else do you notice? Be kind as you explore what is happening.

Nurture. Give yourself the understanding and compassion you need. What is most needed in this moment? Say things to yourself like, *"I'm here for you. It's not your fault. I love you. It won't always be like this."*

Invite self-compassion to step in. This is key: the forgiveness of self through self-compassion. When we show love, understanding and compassion towards ourselves, then we can begin to bring it to others. What happened to you is not your fault. How you respond to it is your responsibility.

When you notice a part of you is stuck or beating up on another part of you, stop and offer some compassion. Say loving things to yourself that you always needed to hear but didn't.

To request a recording of this tool, send an email to **corinne@corinnecoppola.com**.

ABOUT THE AUTHOR
Corinne Coppola ~ 54

 Corinne Coppola has a Master's Degree in Organizational Development and has been integral in bringing contentment, dispute resolution, and job satisfaction into the workplace for nonprofits and fortune 50 companies. Corinne has worked in schools and treatment centers of all types, developing programs and serving individuals and families with a wide variety of needs.

She has spent her lifetime learning the harm and power of invisible loss, pain, grief, substance abuse, and hopelessness. She has walked the walk and brings her experience, education and years of training and personal transformation to her practice. She has helped hundreds of people overcome depression, anxiety, negative patterning, and behaviors to live with confidence, ease, and peace. Through her signature program, CONQUER The Invisible, her clients have gained the courage to take on new adventures, overcome health challenges, deal with grief, take back control in their lives, stand up for their beliefs, regain love and connection in their most important relationships, and more. You can connect with Corinne at:

Website: **https://www.corinnecoppola.com/**

Facebook: **https://www.Facebook.com/CorinneKrill/**

Instagram: **https://www.instagram.com/corinnecoppola16/**

LinkedIn: **https://www.linkedin.com/in/corinne-coppola-5214844/**

CHAPTER 18

The Power of Saying NO

How to Gracefully Get What You Want

By Rika Rivka Markel, Women's Empowerment Coach, Conscious Artist,
Clearing Facilitator

"It's not about saying no to others; it's about
saying yes to yourself."

—Rivka Markel

My Story

I did it again!

My skin curled in on its axis: *No, just don't, it's not good for you, wrong decision, just say NO.*

While this conversation is going on in my head, I hear myself saying, "No problem, I understand, let's reschedule; of course, I can come back tomorrow. I will be there, no worries."

I just drove one and a half hours into the city, parked my car in a much too expensive car park, ran into the building where I was meeting a potential client when my phone rang.

She was so sorry she had to reschedule. If I could come back the next day? Same time, same place.

There I was, standing in the lobby of this high riser in the middle of Manhattan. The whole drive over I visualized this meeting; I saw how she would love my ideas of collaboration, how we would both benefit from this while serving the world, and how our future would be bright and successful.

Well, not quite yet. This scenario had to wait another day. In the meantime I had to deal with that part of me that knew that this was going to happen. That little voice inside of my head warned me, but here we are again: I allowed someone to run over me and take advantage of the fact that I'm not capable of saying no, even when I know it's the right thing to do.

The big question is, why is it that I keep fighting for something wrong, actions that are not helping me to move the needle in the right direction? It's a waste of time.

My desire to be the good girl, the nice person that doesn't like to hurt other people's feelings, schedules, and egos, is not helping me in any way, shape, or form. At least at this stage in my life, I'm aware of what is going on.

A couple of years ago, I was reading a book and the famous quote, "Don't do unto others what you don't want others to do unto you," was the heading of one of the chapters.

While glancing over this, my mind read: *Don't do to yourself what you wouldn't do to others.*

I still don't know how that came up in my mind, but it has stayed with me since that day. I still get goosebumps when I think back on how this hit me.

That day, I realized that I treat everyone with much more respect and care than I treat myself. I would never do to others what I was doing to myself: Ignoring their needs the way I ignored my own, crushing their values the way I crushed my own, and overstepping their boundaries the way I overstepped my own.

If my children treated others the way I treated myself, I would sit them down and have a serious conversation with them.

So I sat myself down in front of a mirror, and I had that conversation with myself. It was painful; it was hurting me to the core. I was in my fifties, and my whole life I lived the idea of "don't do to others what you don't want them to do to you."

Big mistake. My life was all about pleasing the other person, no matter what. Telling people no was painful, confronting, and scary; everything but pleasant and safe.

As human beings, we're wired a certain way. Depending on where you were born, your upbringing, and your personality, your mind will react to the outside world in a conditioned way. The mind has a dozen rules. One of the big ones is that the mind has only one goal: to keep you safe.

Whatever you teach the mind is considered SAFE is what the mind will guide you to do.

Your mind doesn't care if what you're doing is good or bad for you; the mind is just interested in keeping you safe. In this case, safe equals doing what the other person wants me to do, at least if that's how I was conditioned.

When I had this big breakthrough, I also realized I lived other people's lives, not mine. I remember when I was five or six years old, my mother would ask me, "Can you get me the thing out of the thing upstairs?" And I would get up and come back exactly with what she needed. I just knew what she meant.

One day we had visitors, and they couldn't believe that I came back with what my mother had in her mind. This was *the* topic of conversation for the rest of the day. Until this day, I remember the feeling I had, so proud of the fact that I was that good. That day I was conditioned to crave that feeling daily.

I just felt what my mother needed, judging the circumstances, the mood she was in, and what was going on at that moment, etc. I became an expert in feeling and understanding what went on in the other person's mind, and I became the perfect maid or butler, depending on the setting I was in. People could count on me to just get it, *always*. And this became my sense of self. I just *loved* getting it right all the time. For me, this was the most rewarding feeling ever.

When I was in my late twenties, I discovered most people don't have this talent. Most people need a little more information; they are not tuned into other people's energy fields. Not being overly empathic is a much healthier way of being. And even though I knew at the time that it was not ideal, I just thought it was me, and I had to accept it, the good and bad of this personality trait.

It was only recently that I realized that having this kind of empathy and allowing it to rule my life could be very selfish. In my case, it was coming from a place of ego. Not in a conscious way but because of how I was conditioned, I believed that this was a noble way of going through life.

My life was hidden in my imagination, the idea I had to be loved by everyone. Being loved fed my sense of self. I made people happy, gave them what I thought they needed, and resented them if they did not appreciate my efforts. Many times I became the evil one when I finally expressed how I really felt. When this happened, it would come out the completely wrong way, and more importantly, it always came out at the wrong time.

Those moments were so painful; I would feel horrible because my whole being only wanted to please the other person, nothing else. Now I understand that my wanting to please everyone came from protecting my sense of self. Who was I if I was not loved and praised?

The day the "what-about-me" feeling became bigger than the "what-about-them" feeling announced the end of my martyrdom, but also the end of the me I knew until then.

The validation of myself was liberating; I felt it deep in my being. At that point, I thought it would be enough. I understood, and now everything would be different.

Again, big mistake.

It became even worse. Even now that I knew, I caught myself allowing it to happen over and over again. Every time I felt guiltier and guiltier. How could I do this to myself? Why is it so difficult to say no? Do I need this validation? Am I so needy and dependent on other people's approval?

It became annoying enough that I started to say no to everything. This was not the solution. Now I didn't get anything done, and everyone was upset with me. Most of all, I was upset with myself. There had to be a better way.

One day I had coffee with a dear friend and mentor, Ruthie. Ruthie is not only an experienced Kabbalah teacher; she has a feeling for people and what is going on inside of them. Talking to her is always enlightening.

I asked her, "Why is it so hard to say no, and why do I resent people after doing what I didn't want to do? It's not their fault. What is happening here?"

She explained that every time you do something that goes against your values, it causes stress and anxiety. If you do this enough, you'll live in a constant state of fight or flight. It sounds so simple.

I did realize very soon after our meeting that this was easy to say but not so easy to apply in my daily life. What were my values? How do I know my values, apply this knowledge in my life so I can get rid of the stress and anxiety?

In the months that followed, I figured it out.

I found my three core values by going back and writing down all the situations that caused full-blown panic attacks. As Ruthie explained, those were the times I went against my values.

And slowly, I chipped away the ballast that I didn't need anymore.

In the process, I discovered a way to say no with ease, grace, and the result I wanted: a balanced relationship with myself *and* with other people.

The Tool

Anxiety comes from worrying about the future, while depression comes from thinking about the past.

Both processes are caused by being disconnected from the SELF, from who you really are.

Saying NO to yourself instead of YES will disconnect you further and further.

The process of disconnection happens to all of us, and it starts when we are really young.

It's not a one-time event. It happens over time, and it becomes our second nature. And that is exactly what it is; *your second nature, not your first!*

To live a balanced life, you have to get back to your first nature, to who you really are regardless of what other people think of you or who they think you are.

Our upbringing and society are forcing us to validate ourselves using others as the contrast. We don't learn to use our own sense of self to validate who we are.

This exercise will help you connect to yourself so that you can use your inner self as a contrast and sounding board to become who you always needed to become. Once you get to understand your three core values, you will see anxiety and depression fade away. The need to worry will be over, and life will become so much easier.

You will radiate confidence, and a graceful sense of sophistication will cover your existence. Being in this state of consciousness, you will attract so-called miracles. You will just *know*.

Knowing oneself is the beginning of wisdom.

If you ask someone, "What are your core values?" Most of the time, they hesitate and then, after taking a deep breath, will say something like, "family, honesty, and integrity." Or "community, responsibility, and hard work."

It doesn't really matter what they come up with; those are usually not really their core values.

Most people know the list of values, and when you're reading this book, chances are you already did some work on "finding your values." But are you sure those are the ones? Most of the time, we look at the list and pick out the ones we would love to have; the ones that speak to us the most, the values that if people talk about us, that's what we would love them to say about us.

That is fine, but it won't help you on your path of connecting with who you really are. Real happiness and connection to the Universe, being in the flow, comes when we are true to ourselves and in line with who we really are. To accomplish this, you have to be brutally honest with yourself.

So how do we figure out what the *authentic* values are?

Getting the answer will take awareness and time and, most of all, the willingness to let go of what you think your values are. You will need a journal and the commitment that you will do the following over the next few weeks or even months.

Every time you feel upset about something, write it down as detailed as possible.

Becoming upset about something is the first sign that you're doing or witnessing something that violates your core values.

In the example I used at the beginning of this chapter, it would be something like this:

When the phone rang, I already knew something was wrong, my heart started racing when I heard the word "cancel," and I became angry inside but stayed nice to her. I felt betrayed, taken advantage of, etc. Once you do this for a few days, you will find a pattern.

Now you are going to categorize the stories. Put them in three or four categories.

For me, it was clear that *being authentic* is one of my core values.

And because of that, I will be confronted with situations that will challenge me to be authentic and say yes to myself.

Being 56 now, I finally know I can speak up, not with anger, but with grace, knowing it's not about saying no to the other person, but about saying yes to myself. Choosing myself allows me to have respect and human dignity towards myself and towards other people.

In my scenario, it looks like this:

I am on my way to an appointment. Just when I arrive, the other person calls and cancels the appointment."

Now I answer, "No problem; we can reschedule. Let me look at my schedule and get back to you. And it might be better for you to come to me; that will work better for both of us."

I hang up the phone and smile.

This reaction sent out a signal to the Universe that I value myself and acknowledge my values.

It didn't happen overnight, but now, people don't cancel on me anymore. I rarely have to say no to someone, and my stress and anxiety levels became healthy and balanced.

Saying no doesn't have to be rude; saying no gracefully and choosing you is powerful and attractive. It shows that you know who you are and that you're comfortable being true to yourself.

You can find more information (including a list of values) on how to do this exercise by clicking on this link: **https://rivkamarkel.com/the-power-of-saying-no**

ABOUT THE AUTHOR
Rika Rivka Markel ~ 56

Rika is a women's empowerment coach and Clearing Facilitator who will help you detach from your past and thrive.

With 30-years of expertise in holistic tools, strategies, and mindset hacks, she'll help you take responsibility for your life and release the circle of blame and shame.

She started her spiritual journey more than 40 years ago while trying to figure out her place in this universe. She feels fortunate that she already understood that there was more to life than what meets the eye at a very young age.

Rika is fascinated with both the seen and the unseen world. She believes everything is possible, and whatever you see around you is a reflection of what's inside of you.

Rika was born and raised in Belgium but moved to New York about ten years ago. She has five children and five grandchildren on both sides of the Atlantic.

This year Rika became an empty nester. She is excited about this new chapter in her life, looking forward to all the opportunities this will bring.

She loves traveling, cooking and started painting soul paintings during the pandemic.

Rika is a nutritionist, and inspired by her children, she became a vegan enthusiast.

You can find what she is up to on her website **www.rivkamarkel.com**

CHAPTER 19

Trusting Self First

Manifesting the Relationships You Dream Of

By Wanda Knisley, MA, PCC, Training in Power – Level 1 Teacher

"You either walk inside your story and own it, or you stand outside your story and hustle for your worthiness."

—Brene Brown

My Story

"I'm surprised that a Senior Director could have such a messy past. It gives me hope about my future." I heard this from a colleague during a leadership development session who previously struggled with alcoholism. We'd just completed an exercise, sharing what we learned from the low and high points in our lives. I recently separated from my husband and was still raw with emotion. Given I co-designed the program which taught the cohort about the value of vulnerability, I was asked to share early, and I went deep.

That evening, I reflected on some of the comments I received since deciding to leave my marriage. Most were surprised. I remember my sister saying to me, "Why would you leave such a nice guy?" These comments left me feeling frustrated. *We certainly did a good job of hiding the dysfunction*, I thought to myself. *On the outside, we appeared to be happy, and all the while, the relationship was deteriorating for years.*

My ex-husband and I experienced our fair share of loss, including the heartbreaking death of three of our parents in four months. I was determined to find solutions to help us through the trauma: grief counseling, meditation classes, relationship retreats, coaching, addiction counseling, personal training, many of which we tried together for short periods, or I did alone. My ex-husband didn't find such things helpful for him but supported my desire to continue.

In the last year of the marriage, there were endless arguments about drinking and broken promises and their impact on our relationship and family. I was desperately trying to control the uncontrollable. However, the more I tried to fix the problem, the more I was met with passivity and resentment. I was in a space of blaming, brushing over the part I owned as the co-dependent. I rationalized my decision to stay, thinking things like, *I have to keep trying for my children's sake.*

Shortly after an argument one night, something inside me snapped; I remember sitting silently in our front room for what felt like hours. I felt an inner stillness that told me it was time. I silently formulated my plan to leave in great detail. Coming to that very difficult and unwavering decision was correct, although sadly, my mindset was ingrained with the survival-based coping strategies I had used for years. Despite my intellectual knowledge of "putting myself first," I had not yet started to live it.

A few months after my separation, I continued to have difficulty concentrating, feeling tired and depleted. This was foreign to me as I'd always prided myself on being productive and on task.

My entire focus outside of working was to ensure my two children knew that both of their parents loved them. At ages 16 and 13, I found they adjusted quickly. Surprisingly, they agreed the separation was a good decision for both their Mom and Dad to find some happiness.

As I was desperately trying to appear strong and in control of the outside world, I was out of control on the inside. I worked with an organization that espoused the importance of accountability, straight talk, and results. My team and I were falling behind in one deliverable, partly because I was focused on my children and didn't have the energy to go above and beyond any longer. I started to resent one of my managers for their lack of initiative. I had a strained peer relationship: she kept going behind my back rather than speaking directly with me. All of this caused me to fall further into despair.

Feeling the walls closing, I gathered the courage to tell a colleague I trusted that I was thinking about requesting a leave of absence to get myself together. She discouraged me, saying that if I asked for leave for personal reasons, my career as a senior leader would be short. Being overly concerned with what other people thought of me, I did what I always did. Can you hear my inner critic? *Suck it up, buttercup, work harder!* Out of touch with my own needs and feelings, I continued with the status quo, hoping that my efforts to push through would be enough.

Shortly after this, I was let go from my position. I was completely shocked; there was no reason given. I received no feedback indicating I needed to make improvements or changes. The peer who was talking behind my back was there with my boss to notify me of my termination. I remember her smirking after my boss left as she explained my severance package.

As I drove home, I thought to myself, *I cannot hide my pain any longer. Not only has my marriage failed, but now I had also failed in my career.* My inner critic was having a heyday! Little did I know then, having that time to slow down and heal was a gift.

The remainder of this chapter outlines the key practices which helped me in my journey to self first. If you feel like you're surrounded by judgmental people or people who take energy from you—I can assure you—you can manifest the relationships you desire. I did it, and you can too!

The Tool

So, what does this concept of "self-first" mean? When I first began my meditation training, I learned self-first is a primary metaphysical law and love principle in our universe. Only when you love the self can you start to attract this authentically into your life. Self-first is a process of taking over as the leader of yourself. We cannot have mastery over anyone but ourselves.

I was raised to give, serve, and help others. I was overly wary about what others thought or said about me. I felt I needed to be perfect to be accepted. I wondered how can self-first be lawful? The truth? Years later, when I trained to be a meditation teacher myself, I remember the moment it all clicked. We're all perfectly imperfect. We don't come here to beat ourselves up over our inability to reach perfection. We have this life to learn how to attain unconditional self-love without judgment. I can still remember having this visceral feeling of hope when I understood this on a deeper level. What would my life be like if I could accept myself and all of my imperfections? I realized *self-first is not about being selfish. Rather it's having love and compassion for all parts of ourselves.*

While this may sound surprisingly simple, I struggled to come to a healthful loving of self. Why would someone resist coming to a place of self-first, you may ask? After I learned to take ownership of my choices and feel my own feelings, I discovered that truthfully, I didn't feel worthy of living this metaphysical law. While I didn't know it consciously at the time of my separation, my higher self chose to shed the misconceptions that contributed to feeling unworthy. While this type of journey isn't for the faint of heart, it's beautiful, enlightening, and rewarding.

Below we will walk through five key steps to guide you as you make the journey back to yourself. Part of it is taking a stand for yourself, like taking a stand for your own child or a loved one. If you're anything like me, you naturally take a stand for those you love, but applying this same ferocity for yourself is not so natural. Are you ready to take this stand for yourself?

Read through the five steps below and then come back to prepare for and practice each step. The gift for you is in the practical, daily application.

Step 1: Creating a pristine energy field

Close your eyes now and take three deep breaths, inhaling for a count of one, two, three, and exhaling for a count of one, two, three. Again, take a deep breath into your diaphragm and then slowly release the breath. Now take one final deep breath. In your mind's eye: scan your body and describe what you're feeling in your feet, legs, hips, belly, torso, heart, throat, face, and head. It might sound something like this: *Today, I can feel my feet snug in my shoes, I can feel the breeze lightly on my legs, my stomach feels full, I can feel and hear my heart beating, I have a tickle in my throat, my eyes feel moist, I hear a small buzzing around the crown of my head.* Now you give it a try.

Continuing on now, imagine in your mind's eye a movie screen in front of you; on that screen, see a being for whom you feel an abundance of love: it could be your child, a friend, a pet, a higher power. I want you to focus on that being and feel the love. Note any colors coming up around you when you feel this love. Pause here and continue breathing. We're grounding ourselves now, imagining our connection to the earth like the roots of a tree are in relation to the soil.

Now set your intention to surround yourself with white light imbued with the colors you felt or saw earlier. This light surrounding you represents a safe container. A safe space for you to process your feelings and be truly present with yourself. Practice weaving the white and colored light around yourself every day. Set the intent that this loving energy field is always surrounding you. I invite you now to add some light snowfall to your clean field of energy. Feel the coolness and calmness. Now, gently, come up from this meditative state. I want you to write down all you are feeling and the colors you've surrounded yourself with. You'll continue to set your intent for a clean energy field each day.

Step 2: Observe and Learn

When I was going through my separation and lost my job, I spent time in a victim mindset. I was stuck in the blame, shame, and victim game. I felt compelled to make excuses and blame others because I was embarrassed. This observe-and-learn reflection technique helped me acknowledge my mistakes compassionately. It's incredibly important to be fiercely honest with yourself when in a self-first position. We deserve to be in truth with ourselves to admit to and learn from our mistakes rather than blaming ourselves or others. This observe-and-learn technique allowed me to become more aware when I felt compelled to make excuses for my less-than-perfect behavior. Victims don't feel like empowered adults with choices. Victim be gone!

Please answer the following questions while in your clean energy field. When you observe yourself blaming or explaining, review and reflect on your answers to these questions.

1. What does observe-and-learn mean to me?
2. What causes me to fear making a mistake?
3. What mistakes have I made over and over?
4. What causes me to expend energy blaming others or making excuses for my choices?
5. How can I master the observe-and-learn behavior while maintaining compassion for myself?
6. Surface seven answers to this sentence completion. "What I learned about the observe-and-learn technique is…"

Step 3: Acknowledge Your Feelings

I used to be very good at thinking about my feelings, and yet I avoided the pain of feeling viscerally. I rarely allowed myself to be emotional. As a result, I spent a lot of time numbed out and unaware of my own needs. Let's focus on anger. So much anger surfaced after my separation when I started working with a coach. I believed (and many of us were taught) that feeling angry is bad. In particular, our society suggests anger is undesirable and completely unacceptable coming from women. All of our feelings are correct and provide us with useful information. We need to acknowledge our feelings first and then choose what to do next. This doesn't mean we act out irresponsibly on our anger; rather, we feel and acknowledge the reasons we have emotion, prior to choosing how to act.

Below is a simple technique to acknowledge and release feelings, including anger. For additional resources helpful for learning to acknowledge and release your feelings authentically, try Emotional Freedom Technique

(EFT). There are many free resources on this topic which I've found to be incredibly useful. For more information, please see thetappingsolution.com

When your anger is triggered, focus inside and acknowledge your feelings, investigate what's causing it. Notice and name the feelings beneath the anger. When our feelings are intense, we often bundle them together. I used to bundle despair, frustration, or hurt under anger. Acknowledgment helps you begin to release intense feelings. Take note of the feelings that surface over time to become aware of your repeating patterns.

Step 4: Forgiving the Self

As part of an emotional intelligence assessment I completed, I learned the definition of shame is *anger turned inward*. It's vitally important to forgive yourself for the mistakes you feel you've made. For the times you've betrayed yourself. I was very harsh with myself for choosing draining relationships. I had to forgive myself for placing my trust in people who betrayed me. Finally, by owning my decisions, I was able to forgive myself.

Experts say we must forgive others, which of course is important. More than anyone, it's vital to forgive yourself. Let's walk through a forgiveness meditation to guide you. You can also find this in audio on my website: **www.findfreedomwk.com**.

Set up your energy field and set your intention for love, healing, compassion, and other intentions you have in the moment. Remember to keep breathing. Take out a blank sheet of paper and for five minutes, write out all the areas where you've been harsh with yourself, whether it be a poor decision, the inner critic on replay, times when you chose to trust someone and were hurt, or places where you felt ashamed.

Now sit in an upright yet comfortable position and take three deep breaths. Reflect on the paper on your lap. Close your eyes, let your hands rest on the paper. As you do, you might be able to feel the energy from the words you wrote on that paper. If you do, it's completely normal.

In your mind's eye, place an empty chair about three feet in front of you. See yourself walking to the chair and sitting down.

How do you look? Really take a look: do you appear sad or concerned?

As you sit in witness of yourself and feel the heat from the paper coming through your hands, you'll hear me ask you two "Yes" or "No" questions.

If you notice any emotions coming up right now, allow yourself to feel them. You are safe.

1. *Are you willing to forgive yourself?* By this, I mean are you willing to let go of everything you've written on that paper and even things you haven't written, not keeping any part of it for later? You may not be sure you know how, but are you willing to let yourself off the hook? Are you willing to forgive yourself? Answer silently "Yes" or "No."

2. *Are you willing to forgive yourself unconditionally?* By this, I mean are you willing to give up all the areas where you're harsh with yourself, the stories you replay again and again about your faults? When you hear yourself about to re-live one of these stories, are you willing to say to your inner critic, "Thank you for sharing, but I've already forgiven myself and moved on"! As you do that, you're distinguishing between who you really are and your inner critic. In answering this question, "Yes," you're willing to see that forgiveness is not about analyzing or explaining past mistakes and more to do with being able to learn and grow. So, once again, are you willing to forgive yourself unconditionally? Answer "Yes" or "No."

3. There may be something you want to say to yourself right now from your heart, something that you might say to a dear friend. Please take a moment and tell yourself something from your heart: anything that comes up for you (pause for 30 seconds). Now be willing to hear what

your higher self may have to say to you. Create a space to hear it and listen (pause for 30 seconds).

Would it be all right with you to acknowledge that this took courage on your part?

Now gently open your eyes. When you are ready, take that sheet of paper from your lap and tear it up or burn it. To complete this exercise, you may want to wash or sanitize your hands. This symbolizes that you've finished with the harsh judgment of the self, forever!

Step 5: Manifest the relationships of your dreams

Congratulations on doing such incredible work on behalf of yourself! After working on steps one through four for a period of time, check in with how you're feeling. Are you feeling engaged, joyful, self-assured? Can you look yourself in the mirror and say, "I love you"? Once you reach this stage, you're now ready for manifesting relationships from the position of self-first. On the left side of the page, write down how you'll feel, and on the right side of the page, write down how your partner will be. Please note that you can write this with either a current or future relationship in mind. Please go into a light meditative state, reinforcing your clean energy field, and here we go.

When I'm with my new partner, I'll feel... My partner will be....

Read your intention aloud every day or record it into a device and replay it for yourself. Stick with it, and you'll be amazed to see the energy-giving relationships that begin to manifest in your life.

ABOUT THE AUTHOR
Wanda Knisley ~ 51

 Wanda is a leadership coach, executive, mother of two amazing humans, and meditation teacher. As a 51-year-old lifelong learner, she continues to cultivate a more intimate and loving relationship with herself and in relationship with others. Her purpose is to bring the human heart and business together, enabling organizations to become a chrysalis for individual and team growth. Part of her craft is to respect everyone as a capable adult and be direct in communication so that those she surrounds herself with are equipped to make clear choices for themselves. Through transparency and compassion, others will know where Wanda stands and what she stands for. Believing that what you present to the world is based on who you are on the inside, Wanda is committed to walking alongside her clients and peers as they find their inner wisdom and freedom. Wanda lives in Toronto, Ontario, Canada, with her fiancé Brian who continues to grow along with her in their shared pursuit to be at their best!

You can connect with Wanda at:

www.findfreedomwk.com

www.traininginpower.com

CHAPTER 20

Nothing Can Stop My Magical Ass

Creative Pathways for Expanded Living

By Nancy Jones, M.A., Certified Art of Feminine Presence® Licensed Teacher Level 2

"Never downshift to a lower dream!"

—Nancy Jones

My Story

I have leaped tall buildings in a single bound while staying grounded most of my life. There has been a bit of meandering, but always with my eye on my dreams. I came out of the womb as an adult and began taking care of others and myself while saving for college and making decisions way before I was seasoned enough to do that. I was, and still am, not much of a head person, but heart and soul rule in every aspect of my life. I will share a few of my creative pathways with you and then provide ideas about how to unravel old patterns, embrace strengths, connect to Spirit, and create journeys for yourself that expand your life. You will see my heart and soul come alive throughout the stories. Please look at your own life as you read this and think of ways to experience your own personal expansion.

After graduating college, I wanted to work with children who were in trouble with the police. I volunteered to acquire experience but did not find a position. One day I pulled into the parking lot of the state office building in my community, parked my car, and opened every door in the complex, no matter the title on the door, to check for job openings. I opened one door, and the woman at the desk said, "Yes." The position would be working with children that had been incarcerated within the juvenile justice system. She told me I needed a degree. "I have one of those," I said, "and I would like to do that." She said the position was immediate, and I took a state test the next day and was hired. How did this happen? Was it my magical ass? Probably that ass played a part, but it was also a decision to do all it took to receive this into my life, including releasing a belief that it was not going to happen. There was a knowing and a movement within me that brought this into reality.

As my life continued to evolve, I accepted a position as executive director of a large daycare center for troubled little people. When children have experienced severe trauma, extra love in action is needed. My secretary came into my office one bright sunny day and said, "Nancy, there is a man with a gun in the hallway." I asked her if she had called 911. With my secretary lying on the ground under my desk, I went into the hallway.

Remember, I was trained as a parole officer and worked with some of the best diffusers. Every fiber of my being knew he was not getting past me with that gun, and there was not a speck of fear, only determination. I held his gaze, walked close to the front of him and the gun, reached out my right hand, never dropping his eye contact. "Hi," I said, "I'm Nancy

Jones." He transferred the weapon to his left hand and shook my hand, explaining he was here to get his daughter. I put my other hand on his back, helping him turn, and walked him out the front door, explaining the gun had no place in this building. I told him there would soon be a police officer out front, knowing he might panic when the squad car pulled in front of the building. I told him I would explain to the officer, but he would need to go with them. I was trained in other jobs to diffuse this situation. I was prepared because of my choices and experiences to expand my life.

After retirement from teaching, I noticed auditions for a local soap opera happening down the street. That sounded like great fun, so I walked up to the desk and said I'd like to watch the auditions. "Do you have a head shot and are you a member of the Screen Actors Guild?" I was asked. "No, and no," I replied. "I just want to watch auditions." I was told, "You can't watch auditions unless you audition."

People around me were dressed in expensive jeans and berets and looked very Hollywood. So, of course, I, in my non-LA clothes, auditioned for the part of a metaphysical scientist. Not sure what that is still, but I was auditioning. I stepped on stage with the script, and I heard from the back of the room, "Nancy Jones, is that you?" In fact, it is I, including my magical ass stepping into the role of an actress. I'd lived in Sedona thirty years, so I knew folks, and one of the casting directors knew me quite well as a sixth-grade teacher in the classroom. I received a callback that day. Being the quick learner I was, I knew that had something to do with being called back. I found out I had to wear a costume, something a metaphysical scientist would wear, and return the next day with part of my script memorized. I performed and was not selected for the production, and it was an experience that expanded my life. Definition and expansion of self can happen in many ways.

Identifying and deciding not to hedge your bets but stepping into the reality of your dreams is essential to an expanded life and thus a world of wonder and love. I taught fifth and sixth grade for many years, and right after the Pledge of Allegiance, every single day, we chanted together, "Our Dreams are Alive!" In my classroom, there was always an inflated four-person raft. I had that raft in there from my first day at the school to represent adventure, community, working together, and dreams in action, to name a few reasons.

Once another teacher saw my students carrying the raft across campus over their heads. He came to me after school and said, "That raft symbolizes more than meets the eye." "Correct," I said. I had a saying from a Garth Brooks song on my wall. "Choose to Chance the Rapids and Dare to Dance the Tide." That's from "The River." I'm from Oklahoma, folks, so country songs speak to me. Dreams are about chancing rapids and dancing tide.

One day at the end of a very long day of teaching, I received an email from another teacher (Gwen Reynolds), who was to become one of my best friends. She was organizing a hike after school, and I headed over to her room. One of my biggest dreams was to travel the world, and Gwen mentioned she was doing just that. I explained my husband had no desire to travel and money was tight. Gwen explained how she made this happen in her life with no husband and limited resources. I left that hike and applied to wait tables at the local bar across the street from the school and worked weekends at that cowboy bar earning enough money to make the first adventure happen. I traveled with an organization that shepherds children and adults in travel and ended up working for them part-time in the summers to pay for part of my expenses. I've traveled multiple times to France, Italy, Portugal, Greece, Spain, Ireland, Scotland, England, and other places still in my heart. I did not just travel but kayaked under a Roman viaduct twice and stayed in Spello, a walled, Italian city. I love Venice and, of course, the storytelling and dancing in Ireland. So many magical synchronicities made this life adventure a reality. It is essential to note this is not synchronicity only but action-based decision-making to unravel an old, very ingrained belief that *this would not happen*. I had to shift that and take responsibility for new behavior leading to a magical ass outcome.

I discovered the Findhorn Community in Northern Scotland after being hit on the head by a book...literally. As I slept in the private library of a friend, a small book fell from the shelf and conked me on the head. Of course, I read it and discovered the story behind Findhorn. This was in 1976, and soon after that, I made my first visit to this community traveling by myself to Europe for the first time. I was primarily interested in understanding the oneness concept that permeated the Findhorn philosophy and how that applied to my life. I heard about the Transformation Game that was happening there at that time. It interested me and piqued my imagination.

Many years later, synchronicity (my stepson's moving to Scotland) brought me an opportunity to visit Findhorn at the exact time a seven-day version of the Transformation Game was being facilitated. I signed up. My intention was to "unblock anything in the way of me achieving my life purpose."

That is a tremendous intention that I addressed with every fiber of my being. You can feel shifts as you play the game.

This exceptional experience and watching my own life unfold filled me with the desire to bring the Transformation Game to others. Now, I facilitate people in individual and group games around the world. I've developed an internet version of the game and continue to support people from their location online. They often become repeat participants because the game insights are so beneficial to their life's journey.

Stepping out into the unknown requires courage, faith, and most of all, THE DECISION to do it. Each of these life experiences I shared may seem insignificant when looked at separately. But each one helped my heart and soul grow and is one of the underlying foundations for my magical growth journey.

The Tool

Many people seem to be more frustrated than ever these days. We pursue our dreams, but it's hard to keep going when we feel like we keep hitting roadblock after roadblock. We might even feel like our dreams have dissolved. I understand your feelings, but those feelings do not serve our next steps to be our best selves and create a better world. Downshifting to a lower dream is never the answer. It supports a smaller you.

The Transformation Game is the tool I use to help people transform their inner lives, which affects every aspect of their outer life. This game was developed in Scotland and has been available to play for over forty years. It is a fun, challenging board game that literally guides you through a process of transformation.

Remember I talked earlier about my passion for helping people realize dreams? This game enables you to investigate internal and behavioral choices as you explore patterns that no longer serve the direction you'd like to go. Blocks are revealed, personal strengths are realized, and there is a spiritual component that supports the process of unraveling and discovery. You may play this insightful game on your own or with a facilitator. Through the rolling of dice and the drawing of cards, you are shown setbacks, which usually reveal blocks that can get in the way of intention.

Insights come in the form of strengths, and there is a spiritual component to the game that supports the entire process. Since the game has been around for so many years, maybe you have played with friends. It can be played in a superficial-information way or a deeper changing-the-pattern-of-being-yourself way.

When you play with me as a facilitator, I hold the energy to reveal the highest truth. Because of who I am, my training, and varied life experiences, I can hold your hand or kick you in the behind as you walk through blocks. I support embracing unrealized strengths and receive angelic support as you unravel pathways that no longer serve and step into miracles. Being a facilitator of this game is not coaching but supporting in an empowering way with choreography that underlies the process. I've seen this elevate the game to an even higher level of awareness. I can and will hold your feet to the fire, supporting you through the transformational journey to stay focused and ask questions to move you through the process. I help you investigate the possibilities going beyond the known or familiar. Sometimes we connect to past generations, and it is possible to creatively shift dimensions.

Can I Make Magical Ass Changes without a Game or Facilitator?

Without a Transformation Game or a facilitator, is it possible to go inside and walk yourself through the process of transformation? Yes, of course, and that is important to know. Begin in a sacred space with the following gratitude prayer: *Dear Angels of Light and Spirit Guides, thank you for your magic, your wisdom, and your healing in this Spiritual experience.* Or use any sacred gratitude prayer you choose. Journal, meditate, explore your inner light and create a sanctuary. This exploration is not about ego but about the decision and choosing an intention that supports you and your growth.

With this clear decision, do not hedge your bets. In other words, watch out for old patterns of sidestepping and moving away from your desire. Ways of bypassing include saying, "it will happen if the stars align." No, in this miracle transformation process, it has already happened.

Without a game to guide, you ask your angels and spirit guides to actually put you in a space where you can see, feel, hear, and totally experience your strongest desire. Go to that space; call it in with your best imagination. Be clear, specific, and let it come alive all around you and in your body.

Remember, in my classroom, the students chanted, "Our Dreams are Alive" every morning. Yell it, chant it, be the dream. I believe the Transformation Game is not really a game but an energetic guided experience of discovery. Set this up for yourself in your own home every morning. Go to your desire and make it real. As you see yourself sidestepping, blocking, or not holding your highest good, move out of that quickly, cleanly, and with gratitude. You can do it! Kick your own behind with spiritual support!

The game, or this magic process, supports people like us, who want, without barrier or restriction, to live our most whole possible lives. Be sure to affirm your path in a way that increases confidence, clarity, and commitment highlighting pathways and untangling patterns that no longer serve your highest dream. Each person plays with an individual intention.

A few current intentions are as follows:

- I intend to release limiting fears, programs, and beliefs and draw into us all the money for all the "things."
- I intend to honor my wisdom vibrantly living in a beautiful, tranquil, magical environment.
- I intend to embrace patience and inspired presence loving my family and myself.
- I intend to receive my sexy, loving, committed life partner. (This is mine.)

- I intend to embrace my wisdom, strength, clarity, and self-love as I make aligned decisions.
- I intend to receive $1,500,000 in 2021 through evolved authentic, empowered action.
- I intend to be front and center, being my bold self.
- I intend to realize and act on my desires with steadfastness, confidence, and certainty.
- I intend to listen and trust no matter what.

These are just a few examples of courageous, heartfelt intentions. You may be surprised that money is mentioned in a few of these. As you know, money is a form of energy, and in these cases, the people chose to highlight that desire.

A facilitated individual game takes two to four hours, and a four-person group game lasts around nine hours. Time flies by as information is revealed, but it is a commitment. I have developed and now facilitate an online game with as many as six people from six different areas at one time. A six-person game usually lasts a day and a half. Many combinations of people and numbers are possible. Six is the most I play at one time.

My personal intention of, "I intend to receive my sexy, loving, committed life partner," I processed without Transformation Game help. So, just like you might do, I put myself in a sacred space and began. Every morning I took time to look at blocks and the magic of me. We all know we have old beliefs that don't support our new intention. If you remember, I have a magical ass, and I am ready to release those beliefs that do not serve me. I listed conviction after confidence stepping into my magical ass behavior. I know he has already arrived; not sure I have seen his body yet. I revealed many negative comments I was telling myself. For example, I said over and over I *would never find him*. How did that serve me? It kept me small, and, like you, I am anything but small.

Information from the Transformation Game swirls and deepens as the game information lands in the body, so it is not a one-shot thing. Many of my people have played multiple times. After the game, there is a follow-up session to support the person taking the information received out into the world. Angels, insights, and setbacks are selected to underly new details.

I believe this world actually belongs to people who are ready to make their dreams come true—stepping into new situations, unraveling life patterns, stepping into a new you, and not just dreaming but dreaming magical ass dreams that empower and support a more significant you. Never downshift to a lower dream.

ABOUT THE AUTHOR
Nancy Jones ~ 74

I've always had a passion for encouraging dreams in others and myself. When talking on stage, I remind listeners, "Never downshift to a lower dream!" Throughout my life, in every career, that concept has been front and center.

Historically, I've directed three non-for-profit service agencies, co-owned several businesses, and owned one myself. I've been a parole officer, counselor, university professor, teacher, waitress, student, clog dancer, ski bum, and janitor...but not in that order.

I retired from teaching fifth and sixth grade in 2008 and became a facilitator for The Transformation Game in 2011. I decided to develop a business with dream potential at the center and use the Transformation Game to bring that to life. Being a facilitator for the Game allows me to travel the world and provide a tool that helps people embrace a creative pathway that supports insight, joy, and transformation.

In every career I've chosen, I've worked with a wide variety of people, which is essential to me. Most of the people I work with now have been on a personal and spiritual development path for quite a while, and I feel blessed to work with some of the most conscious, courageous, grounded, and loving people on the planet.

I'm currently writing a children's novel about a child with significant medical issues. As dreams come alive for this child, he learns to connect to his higher power to navigate life. Fairies, nature, and love in action are a big part of this visionary fiction book. If I can imagine it, I can create it. "Never downshift to a lower dream."

Visit **www.transformationsedona.com** to register for a game or sign up for a free 30-minute Dream Dive with Nancy.

CHAPTER 21

Confidence From the Heart

Affirming your I-ness

By Pat Perrier, MA, MBA, E-RYT

"You are good enough. Actually, you're probably overqualified, but let's start the day off humble."
—Author Unknown

My Story

I distinctly remember the day I grabbed my cardiologist's tie. Well, technically, he's a cardiac electrophysiologist, but nonetheless, I grabbed his tie.

In my late 40s, I'd often wake my husband, a former EMT, from sleep, saying, "There's something wrong with my heart." Patiently, he would check my pulse, talk me down off the ledge, and roll over back to sleep; I often stayed awake deep into the night listening to a heart that just didn't seem right. I'd routinely talk to my gynecologist, whose favorite phrase was,

"Well, women your age..." followed like clockwork by some platitude or other. Often, he used his own wife as an example. I felt sorry for his wife.

I didn't actually go into menopause till I was 57. Yeah, I know – an over-achiever to the last. My mom told me that menopause in the family generally happened in the early 50s. My sister entered menopause in her 50th year. Not me. I just kept on going. My primary care physician, at my physical in my 56th year, jokingly said, "Good God, you could have a baby." I told him that most women my age, who've already raised families, would be perfectly happy strangling him at the thought...and I meant it.

I guess it was good that it took so long. I have great bone density. But the period of perimenopause sucked. No other word for it...It started in my 40s and Just. Kept. Going. The mood swings. The "surprise" periods. On top of that, the cramps (mine were special: back cramps). Hot flashes. Weight gain. You name it.

And then, the cherry on top of the sundae: atrial fibrillation. But I didn't know that was an issue because the gynecologist told me that irregular heartbeats are often part of perimenopause and menopause. Because, of course, nothing else is going on, right?

This dance of "wake the husband, worry about the heart" went on for a couple of years. Until finally, one day, I was at work. I felt really, really weird, like my chest was sloshing. So I did something that I probably shouldn't have done: I took a yoga pose called Viparita Karani, or "legs up the wall." I was dizzy, and I thought, *okay, let's raise my legs so that we get blood flow to the brain. Putting that yoga training to good use*, I reasoned. Well, the person who cleaned the office found me in that position, and I'm afraid I scared the daylights out of her. I got up, the sloshing got worse and I called my husband. I thought I said, "I think you need to take me to the hospital." He heard something akin to the adult in a Peanuts cartoon: "I wah-wah-chest wah, sick wah wah." In other words, I was slurring words and not making sense. He thought I was having a stroke.

He took me to the local emergency room (in retrospect, yes, I should have called an ambulance...hindsight is certainly 20/20), and since I was pale and sweating, I got right in. It took them 14 hours to get my heart back to beating normally.

After seeing the family cardiologist and having a couple of tests, I got a prescription. A few months later, it happened again, took a day to get it back in rhythm, and I got another prescription. That happened twice more, and by now, I'm in my mid-50s. I had "flunked" four major medications that were supposed to keep my heart in rhythm. Normally, a surgical procedure is done on much older folks. But at the rate I was going, my heart was misbehaving so often, my doctor was afraid I'd have major heart damage, if not a stroke if it wasn't taken care of pronto. I was scheduled for a PVI (Pulmonary Vein Isolation), a type of cardiac ablation. I was young for it, but out of options.

A little biology: According to research from the National Institutes of Health (US), atrial fibrillation is the most common heart rhythm ailment in men and women worldwide, and while the rate of A-fib for women is lower, we have more (and more atypical) symptoms. There's also something called "estrogen-associated electrical differences." The prognosis isn't great: higher risk of stroke, increased risk of heart attacks, and a higher rate of mortality. This could be because of several things: women's symptoms are often ignored. Our symptoms are "atypical" insofar as doctors may not recognize them for what they really are. And often, we've been conditioned that "things go wonky in menopause." So we *expect* to feel off and aren't surprised when that happens.

The PVI is done via the femoral arteries, in which a catheter is used, as opposed to opening up your chest. It scars or destroys certain tissues in your heart that cause the abnormal rhythm. The pulmonary veins bring the oxygen-rich blood to your heart from your lungs; the PVI helps reduce the symptoms of A-fib (normally, A-fib affects the upper chambers of the heart).

Back to my tie-yanking incident. My cardiologist wasn't doing the procedure; this was being handed to his younger associate, who was quite a rising star in the field. I had a couple of consultations with him, and ultimately, he and my cardiologist recommended that it was indeed time to just buckle down and get the procedure done. There was no more that modern pharmacology could do for me, and the risks were only going to climb.

Dr. B (as I'll call him) has a bedside manner that can generously be called "absent." But he knows what he's doing. I trusted his skill; he'd done many of these procedures. I've known the cardiologist for many years: he's treated several relatives for various heart-related problems, and if he said Dr. B was good, well, then Dr. B was good. Bonus: my sister worked in that cardiology office. She said he was good. I trust my sister's judgment because she's been a cardiac ICU nurse for almost 20 years. She can read a doctor like I can read a sentence for proper construction and grammar.

The problem with Dr. B was that he talked a mile-a-minute. I'm pretty speedy myself, but he even outpaced me. Couple that with the complexity of the procedure, the fact that I was very depressed because of even *having* A-fib this severely, and my general terror of surgery (I go under anesthesia really well; it's the coming back that's a bit dicey), it was easy to be overwhelmed.

I had, of course, my sister and my husband to support me. But I was angry. I'm a yoga teacher for the love of heaven. I don't smoke. I don't drink alcohol. I don't generally eat badly, am mostly vegetarian (though I have an awful sweet tooth), and am fairly active. I meditated, I rode my bike regularly for fairly long distances. I knit and play guitar for relaxation, and I sing (good lung power). I don't even cuss! *What was this betrayal by my heart? How could I be so fundamentally flawed (sick, damaged) without anyone paying attention?* I mean, I'm super-aware of my body and what it's telling me. But somehow, nobody with an MD was listening when I tried to explain what was going on inside.

And I was also angry at the doctors who ignored me for years. Years. "Oh, it's your time of life" became a mantra that I didn't want to hear another doctor utter to me, ever again.

On the final appointment before the procedure, Dr. B was going over things and was very excited because he would be using a new probe; his speech got even faster, and I couldn't understand what he was saying.

I grabbed his tie and yanked (lightly). "Stop," I said firmly. He did, though his eyes widened a bit. I let go. I said, "Look, Doc, I'm 53 years old, scared stiff, and I can't understand you. If this is how you talk to a patient who's 20 or 30 years older than I am, and if they're as scared as I am, you're not doing anyone any favors. Please. Slow down."

Surprisingly, he did. He answered all my questions. I felt like I had a handle on it.

Later that evening, my sister called me. "What exactly did you do to Dr. B when you saw him today? He came out of the room with his eyes big as dinner plates and was really quiet the rest of the afternoon." I explained what I did, and after she got done laughing at my sheer audacity, she said, "Well, he probably needed that because a few patients have said they couldn't get him to answer their questions. So, thanks."

I was lucky. I had a pretty good sense of my I-ness. By this, I mean that I understood that if I was going to consent to anything, I had to be confident in myself to ask questions and not just go along meekly with the person in the white coat.

But society seems determined to keep us off-kilter. Just look at social media: "The 10 Fashions Women Over 50 Should Ignore," or "How to Get a Beach Body After 40," and my favorites are usually the ones implying fulfillment with a sparkling clean, *au courant* designer-decorated house. In my house, we have three large, hairy dogs. Dog hair is somewhat of an accessory here.

We're told we need to be "more" of X, Y, Z and less of the "I" – that which we are. The marvelous, wonderful, and wonder-filled being that we are, having the grace and wisdom of age and experience. We have to comply. We have to fit in because otherwise, we're too much. "Too loud," or "too opinionated," or "too brash." What is brash? Who decides what is loud or what is opinionated, and when it's "too much" of either of those?

We do. We reclaim our I-ness. We listen. We discern. We research. We don't go along blindly just because someone says something. We take charge of ourselves and our Self. It's up to you to decide to do so, and frankly, taking any of the chapters of this book to heart is helpful in that process. We practice radical acceptance: embrace and learn from the sucky stuff as well as the radiantly amazing stuff we learn about ourselves.

I'm not saying, "toss medical advice out the window." I'm also not suggesting you yank your doctor's tie. That was sheer frustration. I'm saying, learn YOU. Figure out what's normal for you. Find medical professionals who'll listen to and work with you and will help advocate for you when necessary.

I didn't start out this way. I was a Very Good Girl. I did everything I was told to do. I complied. I hushed. I kept my opinions to myself. I went to college, studied majors that were "practical" rather than what my heart wanted to do (though, honestly, I never really ASKED myself what I wanted – I did what I was told), I got married and produced the requisite two kids. Got a job. I had a career that was mainly in male-dominated fields, where once again, I had to fit in. I was always told, "When you get older, you can…"

Then, I got older. Right about my mid-40s, I was fed up. I was tired of putting a bushel basket over my light. I decided then and there that I was now "old enough."

The sense of freedom was rather intoxicating. And I admit, I had to learn how to use this much feminine power; it took a while to figure out and refine my new skills. I found my heart's desire, and I'm doing that now. Not regretting a single bit of education that came before because I believe all life skills, all learning, has value. You'll know what to keep and what to discard, and all of that comes with age and experience.

Strangely enough, "I-ness" is often not the goal in yoga. In yoga, we aim toward uniting with the Universe, quieting the ego, and attaining peace. We seek *samadhi* (contemplation) and the ability to finally discern between the real and the unreal.

One of my most powerful tools is meditation. According to B.K.S. Iyengar, in whose lineage I'm trained, what we call "meditation" here in the West isn't true meditation. But in my research, I believe these tools can bring us closer to the yogic ideal of meditation if we so choose. And that's the cool thing. We get to make the choice. Take this tool below and use it. See if it resonates with you. If it does, that's great! If it doesn't, that's also great – because you tried it and learned whether it works for you or not. Both of those realizations are valuable.

The Tool

As a yoga and meditation teacher, one of my favorite things is giving students new tools to work with. One of the first mantra meditations I was introduced to in my yoga training was the "So Ham" meditation.

In Sanskrit, "So Ham" (pronounced "So Hahm") means "I am." Full stop – "I am." A full sentence bursting with affirmation and positivity. Easy to pronounce. Easy to remember. Easy to practice.

Set up

Find at least five minutes of uninterrupted time and a quiet place. Ideally, you can work up to 15 minutes (or more – it's up to you) for this meditation, but take it in small bites.

On your phone, have a meditation app; there are many good free ones, so pick one where the sound is pleasing to you and which will gently call you back – not like a kitchen timer. Set it just before you're ready to take your first few breaths. If you're a person who likes to journal, have a pen and journal handy for afterward.

Take a seat. It's best to do these meditations sitting up until you have a well-established practice. It's too tempting to fall asleep if you're reclined. You may sit in "easy seat" (criss-cross applesauce, as it's known by grand-parents and grandkids everywhere) or sit in a chair. If you sit on the floor, have a blanket or towel under your seat; make sure your knees are in line with, or lower than, your hips. If you find this too distracting, then take a chair – the result is the same; only the location has changed.

In a chair, make sure your feet reach the ground; if they don't, then place a cushion or a couple of blankets (beach towels work great here, too) under your feet. You want that connection with the earth. Your posture should be upright; knees level with your hips. Your ear canal should be lined up with the top of your shoulder and shoulder lined up with the top of your hip. Your back is slightly away from the back of the chair and allowed to find its natural curves; imagine your head reaching up toward the sky and your feet anchoring to Mother Earth. She'll hold you safely.

Your hands rest comfortably in your lap. Close your eyes softly, or direct your gaze slightly downward and about six feet ahead of you, "disconnecting" your eyes, so your gaze is soft. If your eyes are unfocused, your brain settles down – it has nothing to concentrate on, no stories to distract you.

Take a few deep breaths, filling your lungs, but easily – no force here. Sigh the breath out.

Let's begin: On an inhale, mentally say *So* as the air comes in your nostrils. Bring your awareness to that inhale; it's going up toward the center of your brain and then into the center of your body. Stay for a fraction of a second – let that fraction of a second just happen; no clenching the breath or forcefully closing off the throat. Then on the exhale, feel the air releasing, as you say in your mind, *Hahm.*

Don't worry about the length of your breath...short or long is immaterial. It doesn't matter if the gap is there; it'll come in time.

Imagine the breath making a circle, in and out. In and out. An easy pace, no stress here. Absorb the truth of So Ham; I am. I am. I. Am. Like a heartbeat.

When your timer goes off, release the mantra to the Universe. Take a few more deep breaths, allowing the vibration of the mantra to settle into your body. Then gently open your eyes. Check in with your physical body and with yourself emotionally. How do you feel? You can journal, if this is helpful to you, for however long you need to encapsulate your experience.

Enhancement: You can add a word to the end of the "I am." For example: confident, aware, loved, joyful, present; any simple phrase that affirms your I-ness. If you have crystals that you like, you might try holding one in each hand. Their gentle weight can also help with the feeling of grounding.

The beauties of this practice are many. Focusing on your I-ness is important. That I-ness is your Divine Feminine, your goddess, your piece of the universal Self. Eventually, you'll notice that gap – that space where thought actually stops. The gap isn't often large, and it takes time to cultivate. And when it happens, even for a slight second, it's magical.

Have patience. Remember, "this is a practice, not a perfect." Each time you practice, you gain an insight. Sometimes, that insight is, *"wow, this was awful."* Sometimes, *"where did the time go?"* By continuing to practice, with intention and attention, you'll reap the benefits of this simple, accessible meditation. May it be of service to you. Namaste.

ABOUT THE AUTHOR
Pat Perrier ~ 63

Pat Perrier, MA, MBA, E-RYT, is a lifelong learner who has held positions in the corporate world, legal field, healthcare, copy editing, and non-profit sector. She earned her MA in organizational development and MBA with a concentration in marketing. She's online at www.elephant-journal.com (search for The Vestal Vegan). She's also an author in the *Ultimate Guide to Self-Healing* series, *Volume 3.*

Her hobbies include knitting, baking far too many Christmas cookies, and experimenting with vegetarian and vegan recipes. She also enjoys reading, classic movies, biking, working with her Siberian Husky Raisa as a "comfort dog" at the local university, photography, and singing in her church choir with her husband, where she occasionally plays guitar. She volunteers as an election judge and is also active in community affairs.

She and her husband live with their three dogs, as "happy and busy empty-nesters."

She owns and teaches at Just Breathe Yoga Studio in Crest Hill, IL. She also teaches workshops, private lessons, and prefers a "functional" approach to yoga – combining Iyengar-based alignment principles with poses incorporating normal daily movement, so you might find her teaching a balance pose called "changing the light bulb" or having students "hang out in plank" and making sure everyone has opportunities to laugh. Her classes are a blend of breathwork, visualization, joint-freeing movement, and classic yoga, where the movements are deliberate, and the ambiance is informal, with the aim of building flexibility and core strength.

She's currently finishing her 500-hour certification and plans on pursuing prenatal yoga courses, which has been an area of interest for her. She's interested in crafting a practice that helps you move through all stages of adult life with grace, ease of mind, and ease of breath.

Find her at **www.just-breatheyoga.com**

www.yoga.patperrier.com

www.instagram.com/justbreatheyogastudio

facebook.com/yogapatperrier

facebook.com/justbreathecresthill

She's on Twitter: **@JB_Yoga**

CHAPTER 22

Tao Heart Wisdom

Magnetize Love and Attract Blissful Abundance Into Your Life

By Sandra Leoni, Tao Senior Master, Feng-Shui Expert, Soul-Coach

"Say yes to a wholehearted life and realize your boldest dreams. We're all together on this journey!"

—Sandra Leoni

My Story

When the student is ready, the teacher appears.

Laughter echoes the foyer. I don't hear him coming, but his words are crystal clear: "Your heart energy is not good enough!" He swirls away without looking at me. It's 2005, and my bottom lip starts to quiver. My knees feel like squishy sponges. *Why am I criticized out of nowhere?* Burning tears fill my eyes. I can't yet foresee that this is one of the greatest gifts I could receive from a grandmaster. Studying with him for the very first time is the beginning of an incredible journey. The insights that will unfold over the next decade are beyond my wildest dreams. Moving through my purpose-driven fear of not-good-enough to teaching and coaching aspects of universal consciousness and manifestation, the art of Tao master geomancy, and applying deep knowledge of Feng-Shui makes all the difference: to me personally and to the lives of my clients and students every day. When the student is ready, the teacher appears.

Getting lost in life

More punches to my ego follow, yet they are crucial to meet and go beyond limits, remove blockages, reconnect with my soul and trust my intuition.

My entire life, I was obsessed in finding truth, purpose, and meaning. I've tried a million things, collected bruises from ice-skating, and learned the lesson that surfing too far out into the sea could almost end deadly. After finishing college, I learned how easy it was to be an asset manager and that speaking five languages opened many hearts because all humans want to be seen, heard, and understood.

After traveling the world in my twenties, hardly anything seemed to scare me. I felt so much at ease, finding myself way more connected to foreign people than my own family. I deeply honored the different cultures and smiling faces. Waving hands and deep conversations touched my heart and changed my perspectives. But not yet enough.

The flashback

At the age of 33, I've become a total people pleaser with no plan, using the warrior woman inside to shield myself. Tolerating some family members' bad behavior and disrespect, I let them put all their frustration, tiredness and suffering on my shoulders. I'm flexible, of service, caring, but stalling my own needs. Why? *Love*, my inner voice murmurs. *You're craving just to get a tiny little crumb of love from them. You've got to get out of here sooner than later; otherwise, you won't survive this.* Suddenly a total flashback catapults me back into my childhood.

"Where do you go?" I've already felt the wind of the open door, but now I wince. "I leave!" I press my lips together. "You're three years old; who do you think you are? You stay!" My mother holds my elbow with a firm grip. The bag on my tiny shoulder containing my favorite jacket, some coins, my cuddly toy, and a toothbrush hangs clumsily on my shoulder and weighs me down. Of course, I stayed. Even though the little girl did not realize it back then, my soul already knew that I would meet my soul family one day out there in the future and that life offered vast opportunities for everybody. But first, I had to do the work.

The stroke

One morning in the year 2000, autocorrection from the universe drops in quite hurtfully. I wake up and can't move. *Get up, Sandra!* But my body is paralyzed: I have a stroke but don't realize it, nor does anybody else around me. I try to get up, but my head turns, and I can't walk without falling straight back down for another twenty-four hours. Tremors wrack my whole energetic system, and cold sweat trickles down my back. I'm standing far from what my soul has planned for me. Motionless and scared, I won't be able to explore what life could be like. The tension meanders through my brain.

If there's a higher power in this universe, please give me the opportunity to make a deeper impact for humanity and this planet and let me survive this. I was never good at prayers. Nevertheless, praying is the only action I can come up with in that very moment of finding myself in a frozen state and not being able to move. Very soon, my call will be heard.

When prayers are answered

"Stop!" Six months later, I visit a bookstore in Germany and a non-fiction book calls out for my attention. It's randomly positioned like a precious piece taking quite some space in the shop, and, heck yes, it also grasps my soul! *These words make sense! Yes, this is it!* "I absolutely resonate!" I speak out loud, and other shop visitors are turning their heads. I buy the book without knowing yet that the value it will have for me is a thousand times more than its price.

"Bend your reality with consciousness. Clear your energies. Your thoughts define the quality of your life. Rewrite your story! Our heart isn't just a pump! Connect to your heart! Treat it like a baby, and don't forget to activate a heart point in your home!" Our grandmaster, 65, is in top shape. I can still hardly believe that the man, whose book I bought four years ago, is holding a Feng Shui seminar in my hometown! The universe could not deliver more smoothly and easily. It's obvious: Opportunities come from heaven, but it's upon us to bring them down to earth.

Open your heart, and miracles happen

"Besides, your heart energy has increased tremendously," the grandmaster points out at one of our seminars in 2007 and swirls away. Since I've worked on myself and activated a heart point in my home, my life is thriving, and my friends feel it, too. *How fortunate it was that I was blessed with this stroke of insight, which made me change my life.* I'm pushing the edges and try to catch my breath more than once those following years. They're packed with consequent learning of all the skills and traveling to follow the masters. I begin to meet the most incredible teachers around the world. The teachings vary, yet the insights are similar: human beings need vitality, healing, a vision, connection to nature, creativity, prosperity, inner wisdom, and good relationships.

In tune with the universe

It feels unreal when I enter the hall at the master conference in Hamburg in 2007. Studying with the grandmaster ten days earlier, I come across a video of Gregg Braden, and his decisive words left an imprint in my heart. Feeling so much connection with somebody I do not even personally know is presumptuous. But it's worth a try, and I call the universe for help: *Please, I need to find out more about this man's teachings, although I know it's ridiculous, as he lives far away in the United States.* Yet, the strong feeling doesn't cease.

After sending out my prayer, I'm not sure whether to laugh or feel annoyed about my wild thoughts. I walk into the seminar room, where my Feng-Shui grandmaster's translator studies some papers for the Advanced Course. "Hi, Sandra, good that you came to assist in this course."

"Can I share something with you?" I can't hold back. Knowing her as an open-minded person, she would maybe at least understand some fragments of my insights about Gregg Braden's latest video clip. She carefully listens to me, and a big smile appears on her face: "You know, I'll be translating at a master conference in Germany, at which Gregg Braden is listed as a speaker." "What? Tickets, I need tickets!" my voice shrills, and my hands gesticulate. Bold decisions are well worth it.

In the next moment, I find myself calling one of my friends: "Listen, my gut tells me just do it, and I'm going to attend this conference." Ten days later, the airplane takes off with both of us.

A mind-blowing event

Mind-blowing is only the first impression we get of this conference. The list of speakers is incredible: Rupert Sheldrake, Bruce Lipton, Gregg Braden; the 'who is who' among the greatest living spiritual scientists show up. Looking at each other with awe and holding our breaths, my friend grasps:

"Now I begin to understand the work I'm doing as an energy healer, and I feel so grateful that you brought me here."

Masaru Emoto enters the stage. He plays a beguiling song, and the frozen water crystals change their colors into pink and green. "This is pure heart energy!" stutters the guy behind. Oh yes! The magic of life unfolds in front of us. The days at the conference are foundational for me to fully commit to choosing energy work as a serious profession. Since then, I've helped hundreds of people to call in more supporting energies into their lives. Unblocking their energetic constraints has become one of my greatest accomplishments.

When criticism kicks in

"Who are you to believe you could transform other people's lives?" At the beginning of my career, people would often unbelievingly criticize my work. "What? You help people gain more vitality and lead a happier and prosperous life? You build the platform to move their businesses to a much higher level? How should that be possible?"

My answer is: "It's possible by taking advantage of the science of quantum physics."

Till today, applying the topic of quantum physics on coaching and inner work either resonates with people or evokes incredulous head shakes. According to the experience of my clients, 98% of them notice tangible improvements in their lives. That is, if we believe in the process, put focus on our personal development and improvement and show a willingness to be actively involved in the process of changing our lives. Or in other words: Where intention goes, energy flows.

What I have learned

It's 2017, twelve years after my first personal encounter with the grand-master, he stands in front of me, calling out my name. Even though he will turn eighty years at the end of this year, I can assure you that he looks like fifty. His skin is firm and vital. He smiles holding my certificate: "Be proud of yourself; you are now among the very few Tao Geomantic Master Teachers in the world."

I feel huge love and gratitude: There are so many beautiful people in my life nowadays. I fully trust them because I trust myself. As a Feng-Shui expert, I study space, and therefore I know if we build a house, we need a solid fundament we can trust in. To build a good life, we also need such a solid fundament: the commitment and trust in life itself. Being in the flow of life is key. If our energy field is like a roller coaster because we're hurt, it will be difficult to manifest fast and draw in the good things into our life. Going against the flow, our struggling could be high.

How to start the process of being in tune

Which group would you like to join: The group of people feeling lack, jeal-ousy, or inadequacy, the group of "I am not good enough," because staying where we are seems to be less effort? Or is awareness key, surrendering to what you can't change immediately and showing the willingness to change those things you can? You choose which group of people you want to join.

So how can we navigate with grace through challenging times? It's very likely that old pain will come to the surface. How do we stay centered and aligned? To reach this status, our inner child needs to be healed first. It's literally all an inner game. Are you feeling the call to leave your old version behind and do the inner work towards a more uplifted version of yourself? Life is a curve with ups and downs: Some days we feel totally aligned, and other days we doubt everything. Accepting what is, we reach a point at which we can design our life at a completely different quality. Catch the wave, get out of your comfort zone and begin to manifest! Remaining in the permanent fight or flight modus costs way too much life force.

The Tool

How to activate heart energy to attract more bliss and abundance

Here's how you can create support for yourself, family, and friends by activating the inner and outer heart point. Working with the heart is one of the most important approaches to create more stability, prosperity, and happiness in the future. Be aware that it is very difficult to manifest when your energy field is blocked or perforated like a sieve!

Firstly, we have to clear our energetic blockages before trying to manifest or attract blissful things into our lives. Not only the inner energy but also the energy surrounding us is important. Pay attention to what you read, think, say, and eat. Violent movies and bad news presumably won't contribute to our wellbeing either. Good frequencies will, and we are the ones to choose.

Pure love is what it takes: Cherish others, yourself, and this planet. Change filters and accept: The others are not me! They are neither my thinking nor my desires, hurts, and soul. Diversity keeps this universe together, and awareness is the key. Never expect others to redeem you from life. Instead, start blessing yourself! And if I can do it, you can do it too.

Sometimes we just need a little extra boost to shift gears. Own your life! May your heart open to the greatest love; may you be a goddess or god who treats and celebrates life as the most precious treasure by spreading joy, healing, and bliss between all genders.

The human heart is the strongest magnetic field generator in our body, and it's 5000 times stronger than the brain. It's the balance point for our multi-dimensional being and empowers us to love and thrive, be in the flow, act a peaceful attitude. Overall, the heart optimizes our entire system. When many human hearts come together with a positive emotion, it's possible to influence the magnetic field in a regional setting.

Love is an attitude we can choose from within. Our perception of life depends on how we think and feel. Practicing love means having the intention to be in a permanent loving status: day by day and independent of whether a partner, parent, colleague, or friend shows appreciation or acknowledgment. When we're coherent with our brain and heart, our energy flows differently. We free ourselves from the ego loop, and manifestation accelerates.

Short meditation to activate the heart point

Let's do a little meditation and focus on our awareness within. Take a deep breath and imagine being surrounded by divine light and love. Put your hands on your heart and smile. Be in a state of bliss!

Visualize taking an elevator from your brain and mind down through your throat and further down to the thymus gland into your heart. Inhale and feel your heart space blossoming like a lotus flower. The sun is shining on the lotus flower bud. Now imagine a rose-golden light in the area of your heart center. Put your hand on your heart, inhale and allow your heart to open even more.

As you exhale, let go and release any past pains, fears, or tensions into the rose-golden light. Let go of any feelings of not being enough and not being able to connect. Let go and focus inward on the light and the experience of blissful expansion and growth.

Now think of a person you feel has been hard on you and whom you do not have a good connection with. Imagine the situation and pour more divine light into your heart. Imagine the best possible and loving outcome for the person and the situation. Lift your hands and imagine sending divine light towards this person. Then let go.

In the next step, let's bless the world and send love, compassion, harmony, healing frequencies, and happiness to all beings, waters, and the planet as a whole.

Feel the coherent love circulating through your entire being, connecting you with the highest divine possibilities. As you move deeper and deeper into the center of your heart, notice a point where your heart widely unlocks, opens, and expands. Soak in this vibrating feeling of warmth, love, joy, and bliss. And smile! Stay with these warm and blissful feelings for as long as you like, and then slowly come out of the meditation.

Activate the heart point in your home

As within, so outside: Outer happiness is a mirror of our inner happiness. Whenever we stay heart-centered and bless a situation, we claim our power back and shift in all areas of our life. That's when we powerfully attract the most benevolent and highest energy for growth, love, and abundance.

With the help of this meditation, you've now activated and magnetized your inner heart point. Enjoy the feeling!

Like yin and yang, the inner and outer worlds are linked and determine each other. To activate an outer heart point in your home, I invite you to visit my website at the link below. There you will find an easy procedure on how to activate the heart point in your physical surroundings. I look forward to meeting you right now!

https://taoheartdimension.com/en/resources/heart-point-activation/

https://taoheartdimension.com/en/resources/attract-bliss-ful-abundance/

I wish you heaven's luck, divine love, and earthly support right now and for the years to come. Blessings to you and the entire world!

ABOUT THE AUTHOR
Sandra Leoni ~ 53

Sandra Leoni is the Founder of Tao Heart Dimension, known for her skills to point out what is holding you back from real success and deepest fulfillment. Her mission is to support clients and educate students to be in harmony with their environment, gain more energy, and increase consciousness on many levels. She has supported hundreds of people to reveal their true potential and increase success to reach a higher level of fulfillment. Sandra considers heart, soul, mind, and body as sacredly entwined. She's convinced our soul knows the truth, and we came here on earth to experience love and abundance. She trusts in feeling and guidance. Whether a human heart feels pain or joy, it unveils the grade of alignment with our soul's purpose and life itself.

Her healing journey led her to many countries and great masters in Feng-Shui, Tao Geomancy, Soul Coaching and Astrosophy. She healed herself by choosing aliveness and is always looking for the synchronicities life offers. Her ultimate personal goal is to master life, trusting in its process. Knowing if we did a good job and have inspired only one or two others to live joyfully, we'll be blessed to happily smile back in old age, knowing it was all worth it!

Sandra is currently participating in the certification program of Professional Feminine Power Transformational Leadership. She is looking forward to helping women in the future to become themselves fully, unleash their greatest gifts, discover their purpose, create deep intimacy and thriving relationships, awaken their spiritual potential, and make a difference in the lives of others.

Her personal love language includes watching the waves of the ocean, enjoying walks on the beach, hiking in the mountains, tasting Mediterranean delicacies with her friends, having deep chats, dancing wildly, reading good books. She considers it the greatest luxury to listen to the stillness of nature.

You can sign up to receive Sandra's inspirational blog about increasing your energy, feng-shui & personal growth:

https://taoheartdimension.com/en/resources/blog/

Website: **https://www.taoheartdimension.com**

Instagram: **https://www.instagram.com/taoheartdimension.com/**

LinkedIn: **https://www.linkedin.com/in/sandra-leoni-taoheartdimension**

Closing Chapter

"Women are a whole community.
Within her is the ability to create and strengthen
and transform."
—Unknown

I trust you found *that something* in this book you have been waiting to hear. This book is not designed to sit on the shelf. Use it for your personal, golden journey. Let it bring hope. Allow yourself to be curious and explore and feel a renewed sense of *wholehearted wonder*. Please come back to this book often for nourishment; let it get dog-eared and highlighted, so it illuminates all that supports you. Share it with your friends worldwide. Buy it as a gift or donate to any organization supporting women. Create connections with the authors in our Facebook page or write us letters via our publisher. Who does not love a handwritten letter?! Each generation has a responsibility to unite in sisterhood, heal, and strengthen any fractures in the circle of sisterhood. Find safe places to be all of you, to be seen, heard, and celebrated. Please love on your community of sisters.

May you live from your own heart and integrity. May you be the safe haven for others, young and old. May you be the lover for someone who sees you as Christmas morning joy or serenely complete on your own. May you raise eyebrows and kick up any outdated women's age narratives. May you adapt, borrow, and own lifestyle practices that suit you. May your heart open to your own greatest love and the essence of divine creation, however you define it. Thank you, sweet reader, blessings and deep love, Lulu Trevena.

... Does my sexiness upset you?
Does it come as a surprise
That I dance like I've got diamonds
At the meeting of my thighs?...
—*Maya Angelou, written at age 50*

Join The Global Community

On Facebook ~ The Wholehearted Wonder Women 50 plus
Global Community
https://www.facebook.com/groups/154614839857015/

Wholehearted Wonder Womenifesto
This is our bonus gift to you. It is a compilation from each of the authors. May it inspire, uplift, and nurture you.
Downloadable here:
https://livelifewithwonder.com/collaborative-books/

COVER ARTIST
Diana Toma

Diana Toma is a fine art painter, working in the mediums of watercolor, oils, and acrylics. Born and schooled in Europe, Romania, she is now creating from luscious Atlanta, Georgia. Diana is often invited to judge and jury art shows and to speak on behalf of the working artist.

Her artworks have been exhibited in over a hundred international art shows, published in art magazines, featured on billboards, and acquired for display in public spaces, winning prestigious awards. Diana also teaches painting workshops for adults within the US and abroad. Her teaching approach focuses on fast, free-flowing painting release and creative un-blockage. Connect with her online at **www.ArtByDianaToma.com**

ABOUT THE AUTHOR
Lulu Trevena

Lulu Trevena, an Aussie native, is delighted by the mystery and potentiality of human life. She is a Women's Group & Workshop Leader, Speaker, Art of Feminine Presence® Licensed Teacher, Quantum Healing Practitioner, Soulful Living Coach, Speaker, Artist, Poet, and Mother. Founder of Live Life with Wonder. She is available virtually and globally.

Lulu is an award-winning author of the stunning hardcover art and poetic prose book *"Soul Blessings,"* winning the 2018 Silver Nautilus Book Award and the creator of the card deck *"Moments of Transformation"* inspirational daily messages and deepening practices for soulful living and the hardcover journal *"Epiphany Journal and Playbook."*

Available at: **www.livelifewithwonder.com/shop/**

Lulu recently became a co-author and International Amazon Best-seller in The Ultimate Guide to Self-Healing volume 3 - 2020, and Find Your Voice, Save Your Life volume 1 – 2021: books about real women, real stories, that change lives. In 2021 leading Wholehearted Wonder Women 50 plus.

In her 50s, adopting the USA as her home, she shares her global life experience, wisdom, and voice, honoring the transformation of the human spirit through self-reflection, the delight of creativity, and grounded soulfulness. She is a lifelong learner and wonder finder. She is a lover of color and texture. She has created with paint, clay, fabric, metal, glass, felt, dye, beads, paper, and items from nature. She has recently been enjoying the art of crystal gridding.

Lulu works with a new generation of women who desire to fully embody and tap into their inner wisdom from their already rich life and experience, finding the gold within themselves and sharing their gifts to help raise the consciousness of the planet.

She is passionate about shifting the societal narrative about women and age…confidence to do anything at any age.

When her children were young, she trained as a Yoga Teacher; this assisted her greatly in both her motherhood journey and her personal life. As a home birth mother and healthy life advocate, she bought her children up with the awareness of food as medicine and finding inner peace in a chaotic world. She is a world traveler.

Lulu understands the depth of community and the longing that all humans have for connection. She believes we desire meaning and purpose for our lives beyond the daily grind, and she reminds us that seeking is a worthy adventure for our evolution. She invites us to see that challenges and mistakes are a rich fertile ground that always supports growth if we harness their wisdom.

You can connect with Lulu at **www.livelifewithwonder.com**

Email: **lulu.trevena@gmail.com**, or **lulu@livelifewithwonder.com**

Facebook: **https://www.facebook.com/livelifewithwonder/**

Instagram: **www.instagram.com/livelifewithwonder**

YouTube: **Live Life with Wonder**

LinkedIn: **https://www.linkedin.com/in/lulu-trevena-8aab519/**

Other Books by Lulu Trevena

Soul Blessings!

Soul Blessings is a 2018 Nautilus Silver award-winning book. It is a celebration of life that speaks directly to the heart and soul. It inspires us to turn inward to the knowingness of our own soul's divine blessings.

Lulu Trevena's eloquent, poetic prose with Laura Bowman's beautiful divine images make this full-color, unique book one to be treasured. It acknowledges the innate beauty of the feminine essence.

Stunning art and transformational words flow through this luxurious, full-color, coffee-table style book. Hardcover 8 x 11 inches.

A gift for those you love. A gift for yourself.

www.livelifewithwonder.com/book/

Moments of Transformation Cards

This set of 44 cards supports living consciously, releasing outdated baggage, and claiming your divine nature, moment by moment. May these cards offer guidance.

Living consciously and creatively is a mindset that requires repeated actions, focus, and stretching our comfort zones, plus a whole lot of play. Moments of Transformation Cards are an addition to your life's "toolbox," allowing you to make consistent, small shifts, empowering you daily. As you consciously release and let go, you reclaim your divine nature, and your inner gifts can be brought forward more powerfully.

www.livelifewithwonder.com/cards/

Epiphany Journal & Playbook

The Epiphany Journal and Playbook is a loving partner to record your journey soulfully, leading you to the rich landscape of your heart.

Epiphany Journal & Playbook Hardcover is 6 x 9 inches, 212 pages, lined pages with quotes throughout.

https://livelifewithwonder.com/shop/

The Ultimate Guide to Self-Healing *Volume 3*

This book contains the power to heal yourself…

…it's what these 25 experts will give you a taste of. You'll learn from holistic health practitioners, coaches, and healers who specialize in unique and powerful modalities for peak mind, body, and soul wellness.

The authors share their authentic stories and passions as well as teaching transformative self-treatment tools and practices that address physical, mental, emotional, and/or spiritual health.

Most self-treatment books concentrate on only one modality. What you have in your hands is a powerful toolkit and a rare find: the collaborative energy, effort, intention, and love from over two dozen practitioners and healers who've made their lives about helping people like you thrive!

You'll be thrilled when you realize the power you have at your fingertips…

…because who wouldn't want a team of badass healing experts to show them all the secrets to living the best possible life?

Lulu Trevena wrote Chapter 18: Personal Chakra Healing Deck, Divine Messages for Realignment and Empowerment.

https://www.amazon.com/Ultimate-Guide-Self-Healing-Practices-Holistic/dp/1733073957/

Find Your Voice, Save Your Life

Powerful Women, Real Stories. This book contains 24 women who share their powerful, personal stories…

…because when you find and use your voice, you heal, and you change the world.

It is immediately evident that each author is eager and passionate about helping another woman find her voice. This book is about surviving and thriving; each a different story offering you or someone you know strength, courage, and hope. The traumas that sometimes sound impossible to overcome are addressed by these talented authors with a rare and intense level of authenticity and courage. They share their pain and their transformations, raw, vulnerable, and out loud on these pages, so that you can feel the inspiration you need for yours.

If you are ready for a transformation of mind, body, and soul, grab your copy.

Lulu Trevena wrote Chapter 6: Unbutton Your Voice, Finding Freedom in Unabashed Self-Expression.

https://www.amazon.com/Find-Your-Voice-Save-Life-ebook/dp/B08VBXHN2C/

Work with Lulu

Learning ~ Deepening ~ Transforming

Lulu offers Personal Soulful Living Coaching, and Quantum Healing, supporting you in your transformative healing and growth process, so you can move closer to your dreams. Lulu Trevena's passion is wrapping her diverse life experience into events and programs. She is an advocate for women, creative living, and self-expression.

Reach out at **lulu@livelifewithwonder.com** to set up your free 15-minute call to see if working together would be a good fit.

As a Quantum Healer, Lulu's clients have had massive breakthroughs, releasing decades of blocked emotions and trauma. She is available virtually and globally.

Quantum Healing is evolutionary and so needed at this time in history. Our internal programs run our lives, and they need to support us. Often, we are carrying outdated personal and generational programming. It is so necessary to delete and repair past memories, childhood traumas, old relationships, outdated beliefs, and timelines. Through doing so, you allow yourself to anchor and reprogram your consciousness with higher awareness and deeper connection. Quantum Healing supports creating your intentions in the quantum field and bringing them powerfully into the physical reality. Email her at **lulu@livelifewithwonder.com**

Extra Resource for Readers

Numerous years ago, I was introduced to the book, *The Female Brain* by Dr. Louann Brizendine, and the chapter "The Mature Female Brain." I specifically loved that more research is being balanced and collected on females. In the past, for anything related to health, studies were only done on men. I also love the information in this book for mothers and parents, and all health professionals. I do not have an affiliation with Dr. Louann, I appreciate and respect her work. Check her book out.

Deepest Gratitude to...

I express the deepest of gratitude with the expansiveness of my heart for the support that I received in my life to allow this book to come to fruition.

First and foremost, my soul sister friends near, dear, and far. I bow to you, I hear you, and I see you; thank you for witnessing all of me. My appreciation and joyful thanks to Laura Di Franco, my publisher, for her vision of supporting people, getting their words out into the world unabashedly with confidence, clarity, and a whole bundle of joy. Thank you, Jen Piceno, for your love, wisdom, and frequent Queen messages. Thank you for reminding us of who we are and the power of our heart's wisdom. Much gratitude to my fearless editor Pat Perrier, who weaves my words together with finesse; over the years, you have helped me shine brighter and your willingness to support many of the co-authors; we love you Pat.

Thank you for the beautiful job in designing the front cover and the exquisite artwork from Diana Toma, the gift of ease and grace present. Deep appreciation to Alston Taggart from Studio Red Design for her calm, clear approach and designers' eye that held this book in a motherly way.

I'm so grateful for all those women who have come before us, to the guides and spiritual masters. Gratitude to all the way-showers, the leaders, and healers.

Each of you in my own life has touched me, whether we have met in person, virtually or through books, or courses.

I thank God for my direct connection, for guiding me to feel the blessings in my life.

A delicious, huge, big thank you to all the women that showed up with an extraordinary amount of sisterhood and vulnerability, and courage to write their stories; for being in alignment to support other women in their 50s and beyond.

I love you all, and I'm very grateful to be part of changing the societal narrative of age and this wholehearted global community of Wonder Women with you.

I Paused

I put a little makeup
on today
I looked at myself
a little different
Not prettier
Not enhanced
Not hidden
Not fake
I paused
I saw ME
A piece of me
A piece I remember
Just a piece
It Shone
In the remembering
of all of who I am
... as immense as the galaxy
no glitter from the makeup
yet sparkles from deep within
... from the stardust in my eyes
and the stardust in my veins.

Lulu Trevena

Made in the USA
Columbia, SC
11 June 2021